For Karen & Joe

Best of luck, & enjoy.

Carl Renlund

This book is dedicated to Warren.
You encouraged me to write this book
and then, you helped me do it.

In so many ways, we completed this journey together.

Autumn Romance

Stories and Portraits of Love after 50

Carol Denker

A-Shirley Publishing

Philadelphia 2009

Published by A-Shirley Publishing
For ordering more copies of the book: **www.autumnlove.org**
267.210.3101

Design by Sierra Skidmore
Heart Leaf design by Jon Barthmus
www.skidmutro.com

Photographs edited by Rodney Atienza. www.rjaphoto.com

Cover photograph by Keith Angelitis. www.angelstudios.org

Photographs by various photographers (See pp. 124-125)

Printed in China by Everbest Printing Co. Ltd. through Four Colour Print Group, Louisville, Kentucky

Publisher's Cataloging-in-Publication

Denker, Carol.
   Autumn romance : stories and portraits of love after 50 / Carol Denker.
   p. cm.
   LCCN 2009908503
   ISBN-13: 9780615314419
   ISBN-10: 0615314414

   1. Love in middle age. 2. Love in old age.
3. Man-woman relationships. 4. Older couples.
5. Middle-aged persons—Psychology. 6. Middle-aged persons
—Sexual behavior. 7. Older people—Psychology.
8. Older people—Sexual behavior.   I. Title.

HQ1059.4.D46 2009   306.7'084'4
          QBI09-600184

Acknowledgments

It's been a long time since I sat down with Sierra and Travis Skidmore and saw their eyes light up when I described my vision. That was the beginning of a journey along which I always felt Sierra's support. I thank her for her tireless efforts, her patience and her perfect blend of professionalism and passion.

A million thankful appreciations go out to all the photographers, who brought the vision alive. What a privilege it has been to work with you. Thank you, Rodney Atienza especially, for taking the photos to the next level with your expert eye for composition and vision for beautiful photographs. Bonnie Charleston-Stevens, much gratitude.

Nadyne Missler shared her considerable courage and wisdom every step of the way. Big thanks to interns, Eli Pery and Jasmine Miller, and to Helene Broitman, who connected everything from the beginning. A huge thank you to Win Akeley, in whose home I completed this book. Thank you to Amy Shelf for your generous legal assistance and for going out of your way to help find more couples. And to Amy Shelf and Amanda Pushinsky for your loving support. I'm grateful to Sharon Good and everyone else who has helped me along this journey — too numerous to name.

I want to thank Michael Ellis, Darcy Nybo, Diana Rico and Nan Schnitzler, for their excellent editorial assistance when I needed it most. Any mistakes in this book are mine alone.

Above all, I want to gratefully acknowledge all the couples who opened their lives to me. It has been one of the most thrilling experiences of my life, to know you and to hear your stories. You are — every single one — in my heart forever. And that's the truth. — C.D.

Table of Contents

Working Together

Healing

Best Sex Ever

Addendum

Introduction

A heart that loves is always young.
— Greek proverb

Four years ago, daydreaming at work, I had this thought: *You always see pictures of younger couples, but nowhere do you see photos of older couples newly in love. Wouldn't that make an interesting book? And their stories too...*

The idea drifted to the back of my mind. Then one year later, at the age of 62, I met a man online. We made each other so happy with e-mails and phone calls that it soon seemed the most natural thing in the world for him to fly from Denver to Philadelphia so we could meet in person. The night before he was due in, though, I was startled awake: *Where were my slim arms, my narrow waist, my perfect complexion?* Gone. Instead, I had looser skin than I remembered and lines across my forehead.

How do I present this 60-year-old body when I feel so 16?

Then Warren arrived, also feeling 16 in a 60-year-old body. We were soon enjoying a relationship more intensely romantic than either of us had ever known. The attitude that I'd absorbed, that is embedded in our culture — only young bodies are desirable, only young love is beautiful — faded away as I experienced the truth: *Romantic love really is timeless.* Then I remembered my old idea.

As editor of a local newspaper, I was used to interviewing people. I wanted to write this book. But until I interviewed my first couple, I didn't understand what a special journey I'd be taking.

It was a gray winter afternoon in 2007. Facing me, in their South Philadelphia living room, sat Bob and Sue Serra, 79 and 80 years old. As she told about her difficult first marriage, he reached to smooth her cheek and kept his hand there. As he described their wedding six months before, Sue leaned against him and stroked his arm. Then Bob stepped away, and Sue leaned forward. "Did you ever see the movie, 'The Enchanted Cottage?'" she whispered.

I knew the film, made in the 1940s. A disfigured soldier and a homely girl marry. They honeymoon in a cottage they come to believe has magical powers because, slowly and miraculously, inside that cottage, they shed all their physical imperfections and become beautiful. Yes, I said.

"That's us," Sue said, eyes wide with wonder. "We're old. I don't even like to have my picture taken anymore. But inside our house, it's like time was never born. We're like teenagers. We play, we hug, we laugh all day..."

At that moment, time stood still for me, too. I felt flooded with wonder. Shortly thereafter, I devoted myself fulltime to finding couples who had fallen in love in the second half of life.

And when I did — sixty couples in two and a half years — I encountered the same phenomenon, that for these lovers, the logic of time had collapsed. In Connecticut and Utah, Arizona and New Jersey, I heard the same phrases: "I feel 16 years old." "I am finally myself." "It's strange, but with him, I don't feel any age at all." The people who felt this way were ages 50 to 87.

The stories I heard — chances taken, lessons learned, obstacles overcome, redemption earned — began to feel like fairy tales: life stories whose happy endings were love stories.

The stories began to group themselves. There were couples who knew each other when they were younger; others for whom the relationship itself was healing; several who were clear, this was the best sex they had ever had. So I arranged the stories into six chapters, showing the various aspects autumn love can take.

I heard fascinating and moving details about these individuals' lives. Most felt passionate about their children; many were accomplished in their particular field. But I chose to include only those details that helped to describe the connection between two people, regardless of their place in the world.

For me, the point of these stories is how two lives intersected in such happy fashion and stayed that way. So I did not explain how these couples merged their worlds after they fell in love. There were a few outstanding difficulties; e.g., a grown child who remained angry when a parent abandoned a long marriage, and some outstanding joys, like the man who had longed for grandchildren and now had them. But what I mostly heard about were positive and resourceful ways the couples had combined their lives. For those interested, I have provided those details — the "rest of the story" online, at www.autumnlove.org.

When a love story begins in youth, there aren't those kinds of worries. Heroes and heroines of love stories are invariably young. In fact, few blockbusters feature a gray haired woman or a balding man with a blossoming waistline. And that is why this book is different.

Here are individuals whose youth flew by as they chased down careers and children. By the time the couples in this book fell in love, they had accrued not only wrinkles, but all manner of sorrows and disappointments (as well as accomplishments). They could have closed down or given up; instead, they bravely kept their hearts open, and received this gift: a love affair in the autumn of life that illuminated who they were at their core. Autumn love, it was clear, was a perfect lens through which to understand and experience true love, which is soul-to-soul. And that flies in the face of what society has been telling us.

The twenty-nine couples in this book are included because their stories are wonderful and because they represent various locations and backgrounds. I found them by cold calling, networking and advertising. But that doesn't mean they are rare exceptions. Love is all around us.

You may think you're too old, or not handsome or beautiful enough, or that you have too many years of emotional baggage for someone to love you now. What these stories, and I, are saying, is *Don't give up on love*. Read these stories and see that love can and does happen at any age. And when it happens late, there are definite advantages (see p. 123).

If you already have love, I hope this book re-ignites a spark. If you are looking, I wish you success. What I hope is that this book will bring more love and happiness into the world.

It is my pleasure to present *Autumn Romance*.

Change

"I wouldn't have the relationship with Ken if I hadn't taken the time to take a journey ..."

— Sally Landau, story on page 8.

Personal journeys are taken alone. Yet, the couples in this chapter found that their journeys took them to a place where they were ready — in a way they weren't before — to welcome somebody special into their lives.

A personal journey — a foray into one's own heart and mind — is to plumb the depths of one's potential. It's about leaving the false path and finding the true one, where we can become our strongest, most genuine selves.

People in this chapter experienced great change later in life and then found true love. Bob chose an explosive shortcut. Vernon's journey was more like the "Wizard of Oz," ending in the same place and knowing it for the first time. Sally grew stronger in her own practical, upbeat fashion. The way Basia let go of emotional baggage had mystical elements.

Their journeys were varied, but each had the same effect: to jettison what was holding them back from becoming their full true selves, so when the person who was just right appeared, they could be together.

Change is always a challenge. Coping with it later in life is courageous. Everyone can learn something from these brave and captivating tales.

SALLY and KEN

"I met Ken at a Rapid Dating event," Sally begins, in a light-hearted voice that makes you want to hear more. "It works like this: everyone wears a name tag with their first name and last initial. You have just five minutes to talk to each person. At the end, you vote for the people you want to see again. Like, Sally L., yes or no. Ken G., yes or no. Then if two people have cross-voted, the next day they get this e-mail with each other's contact information!

"From the very second Ken and I started to talk we felt at home with each other. We were laughing so much that the woman who ran the event walked by and said, 'Now that's a match!' The next morning, I went to my computer and got my votes. No Ken G!! I thought, *What's going on? We really connected!*

So I e-mailed the director and said, 'I really had fun last night. I met seven guys, never mind only four voted for me, but what I can't understand is that Ken *G.* didn't vote for me.'

"Then I get these two equally strong feelings. One is, *Oh my God. I'm never gonna see this guy again.* And two, *He'll think I didn't vote for him and based on that, he'll worry that he'll never understand women.*

"On some deep level, I think I knew he was 'the one,' so I was concerned about him.

"Later that day, I e-mailed the director again. 'At the risk of exposing myself as truly loony,' I say, 'I'm writing to you a second time because I want you to check the ballots. Just tell me that Ken G. didn't vote for me, and I'll stop bothering you.'

"We both took a journey of self discovery — two separate paths to the top of the mountain. Then we met at the top."

"And the director writes back: 'YOU voted no! If you want me to change your response, I think you'll be pleased with the result ... hint ... hint. And you are not going to believe this. Ken called me this morning and said, *Give me Sally L.'s phone number!* What do you mean, she didn't vote for me! I'm going to go through my whole life thinking I don't understand women!'"

It's a funny story. It's also telling. Both Ken and Sally, after their long marriages collapsed, undertook a personal journey where they found the kind of confidence that allowed them to challenge a rejection that just didn't make sense.

Ken's journey was inspired by the movie "Groundhog Day," which a friend suggested he watch. "My marriage was rocky at the end; the last ten years were a blur," Ken says. "That film showed a man going through personal change to get the woman he loves and becoming happier.

"All the things that I didn't do during my marriage, I started working on once I was alone. I did personal workshops. I learned to dance. I traveled, to Tahiti and Kathmandu, and I asked myself: *What are my highest talents? What do I want to do?*"

These were essentially the same questions Sally raised when her twenty-seven-year marriage to an architect crumbled.

"I made a list of all the things I couldn't do when I was married," she says cheerily. "Each week, I attacked something new. One was Argentine tango. One was going to a planetarium. One was getting in my car and driving to the top of a dark mountain and watching shooting stars explode in the sky."

It wasn't that she didn't feel sad, Sally explains. "But the sadness didn't *define* me. It was just a period I had to go through. I didn't date for a long time. I wasn't ready."

Sally was also out of a job, because for most of those twenty-seven years, she'd managed her first husband's business. "Without realizing it, I coached myself into finding a new career. I made a list of all the things I liked to do. I realized that the thing I liked the most about running that company was getting people to grow, in a loving way. So I got certified as a life coach and started my own business.

"After fifteen months, I realized, I had done some powerful personal healing. Taking the time to heal old wounds prepared me to like myself better. That's when I started dating.

"I dated forty-six men in six months," Sally says. "That's a lot of work, but I loved it! If I hadn't taken that time to reflect and grow, I wouldn't have experienced dating so positively. Even the dates that went south, I enjoyed. Because each date clarified more of what I wanted."

After nine months dedicated to "personal growth and reflection," Ken too began to date; in a year, he dated fifty different women. After a while, he felt ready for a serious connection. That's when he saw a relationship counselor.

"We did some role-playing," he recalls. "She pointed out that my clothes were a little dated, that kind of stuff. Then all of a sudden, she said, 'You should shave your head!'

"'That's kind of radical,' I said. But I did it. Then I grew a

goatee. And immediately, women on the street would look at me and smile. So I felt more confident. I felt a change coming. And the very next thing I went to was the Rapid Dating event where I met Sally. I had never hit it off with anyone so well, the way I hit it off with her."

After they resolved the Rapid Dating mix-up, nothing could keep these two fun-loving people apart. There was soon a new list of things they liked doing, together: traveling to foreign places, cooking, entertaining, dancing (salsa, Argentine tango, cha-cha, swing), tending their garden, crossword and Sudoku puzzles, laughing at their dog — and planning a wedding. In August 2009, when Sally was 63 and Ken, 67, they wed.

"We both took a journey of self discovery," observes Ken, "two separate paths to the top of the mountain. Then we met at the top." 🍁

BASIA and RON

Basia describes a mystical experience she had before she met Ron — one in which his spirit, she thinks, made a brief appearance.

"I was led in a guided visualization," Basia begins earnestly. "And I saw ... a soul circle, of twelve ... beings. I was among them, in about the five o'clock position. I could feel the masculine energy of a very tall being at the twelve o'clock position. And I had this feeling, so incredibly strong: *That* is the person I need to know in my life."

At the time, Basia was at the tail end of an eighteen-year marriage. At 32, she began it with the idea that you stick with your husband no matter what. Her mother had done that; she'd called it "enduring." But when Basia's creative optimism seemed to have no effect on the arguments between her and her husband, she changed direction.

"I decided that I would endure ... but for a higher purpose."

Basia's highest goal was to become a emotionally stable person with a great reserve of peace inside. She started by finding a spiritual therapist, who taught her techniques for letting go of negativity. She went on retreats and workshops. She began the habit of "morning pages," a system of writing down whatever comes to mind immediately upon awakening. One morning, Basia was struck with an image: she was in a hardware store trying to buy bread. *But you can't get bread at the hardware store,* Basia scribbled, suddenly awake.

Soon her morning pages no longer included reports of her husband's misdeeds but were filled with reflections on her spiritual progress. "I think on some level, I was preparing to be the person I wanted to be for my true soul mate," she says.

Several New Jersey towns away, Ron's marriage was also awash in conflict. He wasn't thrilled with the continual arguments — "all about who was right and who was wrong" — but he was in no hurry to leave. Ron had married at 35; he loved his wife and thought things might get better. But after twenty years, his wife left him. She had fallen in love with somebody else.

"I made up my mind that I was going to experience whatever I had to," Ron recalls. "I didn't want to stay stuck. But I was in a lot of pain. I didn't date for two years. I needed to figure out, *why didn't it work and what does that mean about me?*

"I cried a lot. I soul searched. I saw that for me, a lot of it was about bending the other person to my ideal. And I came to understand: *When I had another relationship, I would need to accept her for who she was.*"

About the time Ron's wife told him she loved another man — and released him from their union — Basia experienced her soul circle. Two years later, she moved into her own place.

"It was during those two years," says Ron — the light in his eyes is humorous, a rational guy who nonetheless sees a connection — "that I went through all of my soul searching."

To prepare for his next relationship, Ron made sure to leave his last on a positive note. In fact, he was chatting with his ex-wife just before he met Basia.

"I was complaining," he says. "I told her, 'I've been trying to date for a year and I can't find any women.' And she said, 'Why don't you go to a talk?' And I said, '*A talk?* Na-ahh ...'"

"That Friday I looked at the weekend section of the paper and thought, *What about a talk?* And there was one, on Past

Life Regression, that evening. I figured that even if I didn't meet someone, I'd learn something."

But at the Metaphysical Center of New Jersey, he met Basia, and got her card.

That Sunday, on his way to a matinee in Manhattan, it occurred to Ron that Basia's house was nearby. Heading back to New Jersey afterward, he gave her a call.

"I said, 'This is Ron from Friday night. Would you like to have dinner?' All I could hear on the other end of the line was 'a-bah, a-ba …' She was — "

"I was totally flabbergasted!," says Basia, laughing. "I wasn't thinking about dating at all."

"So I said, 'Don't make a decision! I'm about to drive through the Lincoln Tunnel. When I get to the other side, I'll call you.'"

That night at dinner, Basia recognized "the tall man from the soul circle. Not just his height … his large soul."

It wasn't until several years later that Basia told Ron about the soul circle. By then, he was used to her ambitious ideas. His life had vastly improved because of them.

Shortly after that first dinner, Ron and Basia agreed: they'd been through the relationships that didn't work. They wanted something better.

"I hadn't quite gotten rid of that 'I'm right, you're wrong' mentality," Ron says. "But I learned from Basia. She is amazing."

Basia laughs. "Well, I didn't do all of those years of personal growth for nothing! It's like, 'Okay, let me actually practice what I learned … mostly an attitude of wanting the other person to have the life that *he* wants."

"She means it," Ron exclaims. "Case in point. I lusted after a Corvette for years. I always heard, how selfish of me to want

that. But Basia encouraged me to buy it. She figured out ways we could swing it. And she was so *happy* when I went and got it. The kind of support she gives me is so freeing."

Ron feels freed up to pursue his new business, to indulge his skiing habit — and to throw his support behind Basia, matching her generosity of spirit. "The way we talk everything out, so honestly, it has made me go beyond my comfort zone. I'm open to a lot of the ideas she suggests. Usually they end up being wonderful."

For example, what they do when out at a restaurant.

Ron grins. "Right. Well, as soon as we get there, she'll move the chairs around — "

"I always make sure we're on the corner so we can play cozies," Basia explains. "While we wait for our dinner, we can write love notes to each other. Or we make a list: 'What I like about you' or 'What kind of vacation should we take?'"

This last list has a big heart is drawn on it, to symbolize the afternoons that will be dedicated to lovemaking. It reminds Basia of their first time.

"There hadn't been much intimacy in my life for years," she admits. "I had thought, *Well, body, it was nice while it lasted.* Then Ron came along and the fountains just all sprang up. There were fireworks! I was very grateful, because I had given up."

"I hadn't given up," Ron says. "But my experience with Basia was new to me. I thought I was in love before. But this … this is the real thing. This is what they write about." 🍁

JUDY and VERNON

The doctor unlocks the door to his new apartment. He's just getting a divorce. He has bought nothing for his new place except a stereo system. Hearing music from inside, the doctor stops. Whoever set it up must have left the stereo on — and it's tuned to ... what? A Country Western station! That's for blue-collar people, not me, thinks the doctor. But before he can cross the room, the woeful song penetrates his being. The doctor sinks to the carpet and bursts into tears. "They're singing about my life," he sobs.

Vernon Lee had walked a narrow and circumspect path. His Chinese parents drummed solemn values of honesty and success into him and his four siblings as they grew up in Honolulu. All five were encouraged to "marry white" — in that time and place, it was one more way to get ahead. So when the pretty Caucasian woman he'd been dating for eight months issued an ultimatum — marriage, if he was "really serious" — Vernon complied.

Vernon's office manager and her mother had already agreed: Judy and Vernon would be perfect for each other. "Tell them why you didn't want to meet me, honey," Judy says in her soft, bemused voice.

"My wife used to tell me I was boring. Now I was learning to be interesting. I was learning something else too: that I had never really loved her."

"I got to Denver when I was twenty-seven. By the time I opened my practice I was thirty. Getting married was the next thing to do, I figured," he says.

But Vernon hadn't figured in such matters as compatibility.

"People used to tell us, 'You two are the most different people I know!' And it was true! How we felt about fun, our ideas about affection, *everything* was so different...

"The day after I got married, I knew it was a mistake. The day *after!* But I wasn't going to bail out. All I could think was, I took a vow to spend my life with you and I will."

Eighteen years passed. Vernon got used to feeling lonely. He got used to his wife's criticisms. She was right; he didn't know what to say at parties, or how to dress. Vernon concentrated on building up his practice. His patients, at least, seemed to like him. Then one day one of them said, "Hey, I saw your wife at the attorney's today."

"Honey, were you at our attorney's today?" Vernon asked that night. Minutes later he learned that his wife had been seeing another man and she wanted a divorce.

"And just like that, it was over."

Vernon's eyes are wide with remembered shock. "I'd been a good boy. God was going to take me straight to Heaven. Now everything was turned upside down..."

The pain was so bad that Vernon began seeing a therapist. And every night, he would listen to KYGO, Denver's country station. It was the only thing that made any sense.

"Every song was cheating, hurting, longing — what my life had become. I went out and bought a hundred country CDs that first year. One song I played over and over, Travis Tritt singing "For You." He's saying he didn't cry anymore because he'd found someone to love. I would listen to that track in my car and cry."

Then Vernon found out he could hear this music live, at a place called The Grizzly Rose. He smiles, now, at the memory.

"I bought cowboy boots and the right kind of jeans. I went in and sat down. A song comes on. Everyone in the place *jumps* on the dance floor. They all move one way — then the other — all *together*. Afterwards I tapped a woman on the shoulder and asked, 'Ma'am, what was that?' 'That was the Electric Slide,' she said. 'How do you do it?' 'You take a lesson!'"

So Vernon took dance lessons. He also took up golf, and painting and photography. He excelled at everything he tried; this was familiar. But it was no longer enough.

"When I first started, I took photographs of things other people would think were beautiful. Then I told myself, *take pictures of what* you *think is beautiful!* That felt so different!"

Instead of fulfilling others' expectations, he was starting to feel, and fulfill, his own. Vernon donated his entire wardrobe (clothes his wife had selected) to charity and shopped for clothes that *he* liked. "Who cares if you wear a purple shirt with a brown tie, as long as you are happy," said his therapist.

Vernon was getting happier. But socializing still made him uncomfortable. "I didn't have anything to say," Vernon recalls. "When guys asked, 'Hey did you see what Michael Jordan did last night?' I would think, *Who is Michael Jordan?* So my therapist told me, 'I want you to learn a little bit of everything.'"

Vernon loved this assignment. He started reading the newspaper, followed by *Time* magazine and *Sports Illustrated*. "I sat there at night and learned who were the best starts, the final sixteen, the hockey whatever …

"My wife used to tell me I was boring," Vernon says quietly. "She was right. Now I was learning to be interesting. I was learning something else too: that I had never really loved her."

The thought of making such a huge mistake again horrified him. Vernon imagined he'd stay single forever.

All through Vernon's tale, Judy has been at his side. A light hand on his arm when he described his divorce. Appreciative chuckling when he re-enacted the Electric Slide scene. Now she tells her story.

Judy's parents emigrated from Japan and ended up in Colorado. Her older sisters — all in traditional arranged marriages — felt that Judy, the youngest of twelve, was spoiled because she was allowed to date, like American girls. But Judy, too, had to marry Japanese. At 22, she and Donald tied the knot. But twenty-eight contented years later, Donald was diagnosed with cancer and died less than a year later.

"I was a widow so young," Judy says softly. "I was so alone. "

Her husband hadn't wanted that for her.

"Right before he died, my husband told me his wish, that I would marry again," Judy says. Her serene composure breaks as she reaches for a tissue. "It was a beautiful thing to do. But deep down, I didn't believe it."

After a few hard years, Judy joined a golf group. Then she took line dancing lessons; soon, she was teaching classes herself at nine different centers. She had loved dancing as a girl. Now life seemed good again, even if she was alone.

"I never dreamt I'd have a man in my later years. And then one day in 2005, a lady in my dance class said that she knew a man, a doctor — in fact, her daughter was his office manager. He was a golfer and a dancer, my two loves!"

That was the first time Judy heard of Vernon. But he'd learned of her three years before. Back then, Vernon's office manager and her mother had already agreed: Judy and Vernon would be perfect for each other.

"Tell them why you didn't want to meet me, honey," Judy says in her soft, bemused voice.

"I'd never dated an Asian woman in my life," Vernon admits. "Until Judy, I was like a banana, yellow on the outside but white on the inside."

It wasn't until 2005, when Vernon spent the July 4th weekend with his office manager and her family, that he gave in.

"They sat me down and grilled me," Vernon recalls. "'Where was my *life* going? Who was I *dating?* What were my *goals?*' Then they said, 'Listen. This lady we told you about, she is just like you.'"

Those words made an impression. Vernon now knew who he was. Shortly thereafter, when he was 59 and Judy was 64, he took her out for dinner.

"I saw right away that Judy was the kindest woman I had ever met," Vernon says.

Judy smiles, "As soon as we started talking and laughing, I realized how lonely I had been for someone exactly like Vern. And two months later I was in his house!"

"What happened was, some of my family showed up," Vernon explains. "So I said, 'Judy, why don't you come here and bring enough stuff for five days, so we can just do things?' After five days, I said, 'Judy, we are having too much fun. You can't go home!' And she said, 'I don't want to go home.'"

"We are so the same," Judy says now. "Donald and I weren't this much alike. His dearest friends are my dearest friends. Vern and I golf every chance we get. We love to dance together. Look, here are our certificates! We won first prize two years in a row for waltzing at the Senior Olympics."

This lady we told you about, she is just like you...

"We like the same kind of fun, the same kind of affection," Vernon says. "Judy and I both like to be held at night. She is such a gentle person. I am too. I love to bring her coffee in the morning..."

"Vern rubs my feet! He does everything for me."

"It is easy because there is so much love. We tell each other thirty times a day, 'I love you.'"

"In the middle of the night, I can hear him say 'I love you,'" Judy teases. "He must say it while he's sleeping." 🦋

You've shown me love I never knew / And there is nothing I won't do for you.
— Travis Tritt and Bruce Ray Brown, "For You"*

*Post Oak Publishing; Brass Crab Publishing.

SUSAN and ED

On April 8, 2004, when Susan was nearing 60, she announced to a roomful of strangers: "I want a juicy, succulent relationship with the man of my dreams. In fact, I will be married by April 15, 2005!"

No, this tall sensible blonde had not lost it. She was merely following orders. Each person in the workshop that Susan had traveled from Washington D.C. to Philadelphia to attend was told to state, unequivocally, what major change they wanted in their life.

Susan believed in possibilities beyond what she could see. Her lifelong hobby was sewing small decorative quilts — and even as she grounded her pieces with precise stitches, the "line" of her stitching always stretched yearningly toward the fabric borders.

Seven years before, Susan had left her long marriage, unwilling to settle for a lack of shared values. She built up a good life, with a job she adored and a rich network of friends. She looked at herself and made personal changes. Now Susan felt ready for love. She believed in the spiritual maxim that told her to put her desire out to the Universe.

Her blue eyes twinkle with ironic humor. "I just didn't think it would happen *immediately*," Susan says, smiling. "It was right after the workshop that a woman came up to me and asked if she could give my phone number to a wonderful man she knew."

His name was Ed and he was a lot like Susan. Both had no-nonsense personalities. Both kept their tender hearts hidden. Each had endured personal tragedy. Susan's parents and brother perished in a fire when she was 17. Ed's mother died when he was 9; his wife died of cancer when she was 48. Both Susan and Ed knew how to gratefully move forward, believing that happiness lay ahead.

After Ed's wife died, he left what until then had been his dream job — vice president of a high level non-profit organization — to do something that would affect people's lives more directly. Then 62, Ed started a service: Dependable Drivers. When he first heard about Susan, Ed was interested, especially after he saw her photo. But he drove a thousand miles a week and she lived almost two hundred miles away. So Ed addressed the problem in his typical no-frills fashion.

"Because this was a geographically undesirable relationship, I thought I'd short-circuit the getting-to-know-you process. I sent her an e-mail revealing about ninety percent of my life."

When they met in person a month later, Ed took along a briefcase that contained the rest of his life and emptied it onto the restaurant table. Among papers documenting his work history and medical records was a "Life Values" questionnaire — which Ed suggested they fill out then and there, together.

"Yes, I saw the humor in it," Susan says, laughing. "I *liked* that he was so open. And I liked that our top ten values matched with slightly different orders. That was a *huge* plus!"

But what caused Susan to fall deeply in love was Ed's outsized, romantic heart. She kept catching glimpses of it: when, on her first visit to Philadelphia, Ed packed the schedule with everything she loved: theater, music, beautiful gardens. And when she called him to sadly report, she'd been given a "C" for her first efforts on a big workshop project — and Ed

Leaving everything familiar behind was harder than Susan imagined but it allowed another dream to come true.

sent her an e-mail with a string of "C" words.

"They were all positive, like charming, charismatic, cute, celebratory and such," Ed says matter-of-factly. "I can read them all if you like."

He can easily reel off the words four years later because the list is in his hands. Ed saved everything — e-mails, photos, love notes — from the beginning of their relationship and pasted it all in a scrapbook: "A Visual Journey of Susan and Ed." Near the end is a children's drawing of the happy couple; Susan's grandchildren created it for the wedding invitation.

On May 1, 2005, Susan and Ed were married at the Politics and Prose Bookstore in Washington D.C. "It wasn't *exactly* my prediction but it was close enough!" says Susan, beaming.

They both assumed their home would be in Washington. But Susan observed how much Ed's business meant to him. She considered that a change might be exciting, and decided, *she* would move to *Philadelphia*. Leaving everything familiar behind was harder than Susan imagined. But the change provided yet another opportunity for her to grow.

"Susan," Ed points out proudly, "has built a business."

A cozy upstairs bedroom in their Philadelphia home is command central for *Susan Leonard: Quilted Fabric Art*. A growing clientele brings Susan baby clothes, t-shirts, hats, and other personal items. Carefully and precisely, knowing how precious life is in all its surprising turns, Susan stitches together the past in order to grace the present. ❧

WANDA and BOB

Do you think that change will manifest when you *believe?* Wanda did. She always had. So in 2007, when Wanda was 53 and felt it was time for the right man to enter her life, she took herself on a "mediation walk" and put it out to the Universe.

What she heard back was: *The man is not ready.*

Well, I'm ready! Wanda thought. *This person needs to get it together!*

But since Wanda truly believes that things happen when they're supposed to, she realized she had some time on her hands. She used it to build a "vision board" — a composite of words and images to describe the man she wanted.

"I imagined that he would be very romantic … and educated and good with words. He would have a fun-loving spirit. His house would be open and filled with light. And he would be very open. He would be able to see *me*."

She got it right on all counts. Wanda also heard the Universe correctly: This man was not ready yet.

In 2007, realtor Bob Tracey was not ready to see Wanda's extraordinary soul. He first had to find his own.

The process didn't begin pleasantly. Everything Bob counted on began to fall away that year. His father died. The real estate market tanked. His income plummeted ninety percent in the space of eighteen months. Then the relationship Bob had been in for four and a half years went south. His girlfriend was a gorgeous former model. In fact, every woman Bob ever dated had been stunningly beautiful.

With nothing left of his "successful" life, Bob was at a loss. He went to visit a friend and met another fellow there, who introduced himself as a "holistic practitioner." The man looked Bob up and down and said, "You have a serious energy blockage and you need to have it cleared."

"To me, this was all airy-fairy nonsense," Bob recalls. "Except … the man looked right through me. On some level, I knew it was the truth."

Bob's father had left him a small amount of money, so Bob could "do something for himself." He used the funds for a week long series of what the practitioner called "quantum energy treatments." The results were dramatic.

"I felt a transformation so complete it's almost impossible to describe. My physical being was cleared. I could see better, run faster …

"But mostly," Bob says, "I understood that for all my fifty-four years I had been seeing life through a filter of shame. Toxic shame. Which was now *gone*."

Feeling like a "brand new person," Bob took six months to review his previous relationships and imagine his future.

"My first criteria for choosing a woman had always been the way they looked. Now my priorities were different. I pictured a whole other kind of relationship, one of utter harmony, with a deep spiritual connection."

Just as Wanda had conjured up a man with her vision board, Bob invoked the exact relationship he desired — with a poem.

"The Couples Song," Bob's paean to a spiritual love affair, describes an elevated state where two individuals "banish forever from the sacred space of Us, all blame" and abide by this rule: "Whenever one of Us feels the need to be right, We choose to be kind instead."

If a lifetime of toxic shame could be cleared in a week, then surely a couple could achieve such accord — if they both wanted it. Bob set about finding a woman who cared about peace and harmony as much as he did. He signed up for an online dating service. Wanda now visited that site and was attracted to Bob's profile.

"By the time we agreed to meet, I already really liked her," says Bob, who waited eagerly for Wanda in the restaurant.

"Unquestionably ... Wanda wasn't the kind of conventional beauty I'd been attracted to before," he says slowly. "She was curvier than those model types. But she brought this lovely quality, a sweet calm and tranquility, into the restaurant with her. I could tell she was an extraordinary person."

Bob's newly enlightened perspective was one Wanda had embraced most of her life. One of seven sisters growing up in New Orleans — and the self-described risk-taker among them —Wanda began the habit early on of making decisions that were right for her, based on her innermost values.

A series of brave decisions brought Wanda to Los Angeles as a young woman. Things went well — then at 32, she was briefly disheartened. "I was a single, African American woman, now pregnant. This was not what I imagined."

Trying to decide whether or not to keep the baby took Wanda to a new spiritual level. She realized there was nothing more important than giving this child a good life.

"I didn't date while I was raising my son," Wanda says quietly, "because I wasn't confident I would meet someone who would bring peace into the home. That was my biggest value."

When her son joined the Air Force, Wanda felt free to try her wings again. She was in Las Vegas just a short while when she met Bob.

"When we met each other, I was flat broke," recalls Bob, "and Wanda was overweight. In our society, those are two things that have no value. I think we both needed to be loved for just ourselves. And that's what happened."

As they lived the accepting lifestyle outlined in "The Couples Song" — Bob often taking his cue from Wanda — improvements appeared in their individual lives. Bob's business took off. Wanda found herself motivated to hit the gym.

"One of the effects of this relationship was that I started to love myself more and take care of myself more," says the imperturbable Wanda — who was taken by tearful surprise on Valentine's Day, 2009, when Bob read "The Couples Song" aloud at their spiritual center — and then proposed to her in front of everyone.

They were married six months later. Wanda and Bob now counsel other couples in achieving a no-blame relationship. ❧

It's You Again

Hours fly, Flowers die
New days, New ways, Pass by. Love stays.

— *Henry Van Dyke, American writer (1852-1933)*

The couples in this chapter knew each other when they were young — and fell in love when they were older.

For some, it was the second time they fell. For others, it was a waiting game. Albert was 29 when he realized Mileigh was the one for him. At 84, he set off across the country to find her again. RJ was 13 when he fell hard for Esther. He was 62 when they finally had their first date.

What moved RJ and Albert to pursue the girls they had adored from afar — when those girls were clearly now older women? The answer reveals love's essence: The spirit is what we truly fall in love with; the body is merely the vessel.

RJ disembarked from the airplane with Esther's high school photo displayed around his neck, as if to say, bodies may age, but *It's still you; it's still me* … Like everyone else in this chapter, he learned how rare and precious love is and how far he was willing to go to have it in his life.

These couples discovered love was better the second time around because they had learned to truly value it. Best of all, they learned that love did not die. Love survived other mates, marriages, time and distance.

As one person observed, simply, "Love endures."

ESTHER and RJ

On a sunny spring morning in 1958, in the little town of Dobbs Ferry NY, a slender 13-year-old girl walked to her new school. The 13-year-old boy who watched her approach felt his heart skip a beat. *That's the most beautiful girl I've ever seen,* he thought, as she entered the light-dappled schoolyard.

Esther's graceful walk — the way her huge dark eyes took in the world so completely — pried open Raymond John's heart. He was always called RJ, and his heart was generally closed.

Esther's heart was shut down, too, against a sadness she could never name. She craved more affection than her pre-occupied parents could supply. A rabbi's daughter, the eldest child, she wanted only to set a good example. Trying so hard left Esther isolated — and too disconnected to notice that RJ always had a crush on her, ever since that first glance.

Each went off on a life of their own. Each went off on a life of escape. He continued to try to achieve the unreachable goals he felt he had to in the city of N., while she had the wherewithal to develop an independent life of her own in the City of R., hundreds of miles away.

— A Modern but Incomplete Fairy Tale, by RJ Ruble

The "independent life" did not come easy. Shortly after Esther moved to Rochester with her medical-student husband and small baby, her marriage fell apart.

"I was terrified. Nothing was familiar," she recalls. "It was then that I started to change."

Therapy helped. So did raising her daughter with the intense nurturing Esther herself had always craved. Then, at age 46, Esther discovered swing dancing.

"I'm my father's daughter, rabbi means teacher and I loved teaching swing dancing classes. I found a business partner and we established the Rochester Swing Dance Network. It became a community! People met there and got married!"

Other people, not Esther.

Even in this new life she was proud of, sadness sat deep inside Esther like a stone. "In some ways I was like a human-doing, not a human-being. I was always busy."

Working full time, raising her daughter, running the Dance Network — the years went by. In 2003, Esther was 58 and a grandmother. She started off the New Year by trying to connect with old friends through Classmates.com. RJ saw her name and e-mailed her immediately.

"After many, many years, they came across each other again. But by then they had lived through things that fairy tales leave out..."

At 58, RJ was a successful tax attorney, a partner in his firm, with a wife and two children. Inside these trappings of success, though, he was all alone.

"People would tell me I was charming, but that was deceptive because I never felt any connection," RJ says with a thin smile. "The anger and alcoholism in my childhood made me this locked-up person. To show you how cold I was, when my wife called to tell me she was in labor with my first child, I told her I was busy working. She had to call me back three times."

"But then in the hospital, I held my newborn daughter in my arms and my heart melted. Then it happened with my son two years later. I could be open with my children because they felt safe. But those feelings didn't transfer to anyone else. My kids were already teenagers when Esther and I began writing."

"Our e-mails weren't intimate in the romantic sense," Esther

recalls. "They were a conversation between two people who found that they liked each other a lot. RJ was accomplished. He was witty. But I could tell he was a 'human-doing' like I was."

He was also someone whose life was about to fall apart. RJ had a disagreeable parting of the ways with his firm and had to set out on his own. Under the stress, his marriage collapsed. Then in 2006, he faced a federal indictment for tax shelter improprieties. Because Esther felt like his closest friend, he told her everything.

During the four years they corresponded, RJ periodically asked if he could visit Esther. She responded with her usual caution: "Yes ... in 2007." He held her to it. In March 2007, RJ flew from New York City to Rochester, descending from the airplane with Esther's high school photo around his neck. They were both 62 years old.

"The second night he was here, we made love," recalls Esther. "Afterwards I started to cry. And I didn't stop. I cried and cried, for eighteen hours straight!

"I think it was all those years of being alone, of not being able to share my grief. I would look up and see RJ's comforting face and cry some more. By the time he got on the plane Sunday night, we had barely had a meal and I was still crying."

As shut off as he'd been to everyone else, that's as open as RJ was to Esther. He held her as she cried. Immediately upon returning home, he sat down and wrote *A Modern but Incomplete Fairy Tale* which told, in romantic language, their story.

Esther and RJ cast their lots in with each other; happiness, innocent and plentiful, followed. RJ moved to Rochester the next year and bloomed. "He lost forty pounds, learned to dance and started doing yoga," exults Esther, whose friends marveled at the change in her, too. All the tension gone from that pretty face!

The last dragons to slay were Esther and RJ's defensive patterns of behavior. "It wasn't easy to let them go. But we did it, layer by layer," says RJ. "We wanted to be as open with each other as possible."

On July 3, 2009, they were married in their Rochester backyard. In a child's fairy tale, worldly riches would accompany this happy ending. But... *They had lived through things that fairy tales leave out.*

RJ's money was gone, lost to legal battles. He moved to Rochester with nothing but his love for Esther. Like the princess who exchanged gold for wisdom, Esther felt only joy.

"I always knew I had to live my own life," she says. "What I didn't know was at the end there would be this wonderful gift." 🍃

As the weather outside grew colder, the wall of hurt between them began to thaw. A hug in the hall. A kiss on the cheek. It was love, but not passionate love. But then that changed, too.

BERNADETTE and JIM

Ever since Bernadette asked Jim to dance, when she was 15 and he was 16, they were crazy about each other. Five years later, they married, on August 21, 1964; soon they had two beautiful daughters. Jim worked several jobs so Bernadette could stay home with the girls. Life was so good that Bernadette remembers thinking, *I'm just so happy — I'm afraid something's going to happen.*

The thing that happened was gradual: they took their relationship for granted. Jim worried so much about making ends meet that he was rarely home. Bernadette felt ignored, and complained. Jim had open-heart surgery in his 30s; neither of them enjoyed his enforced stay at home because they were both worried about money. By the time Jim returned to a nine-to-five job, Bernadette was working night shift. Resentments and misunderstandings built into a wall; over that wall, they shouted at each other, louder and louder.

One afternoon, Bernadette opened the front door to find teenaged Michelle, her oldest, waiting to hear if her parents were fighting. "If your daughter doesn't know to come in the house or not, that's not a good environment," Bernadette says briskly. "Jim wouldn't leave. So I did."

On August 21, 1989, the couple filed for divorce. "It was heartbreaking. That was our twenty-fifth anniversary," says Jim. He longed for Bernadette for two years; then he faced reality. She had a boyfriend; soon, he had a girlfriend. In ten years,

they saw each other only twice, at their daughters' weddings.

Then, when Jim was 54, they needed to see each other face to face. His inherited kidney condition had kicked in a while back but now the doctor was clear: without a kidney, Jim would die. Family members were tested. His ex-wife was a perfect match.

Bernadette dug deep in her heart. She concluded that Jim *deserved* her kidney. "When my daughters were small, this man worked two and three jobs. He let me stay home and be their mom. I felt it was only fair that Jimmy be around, to get the love he had earned."

Tears streamed down Jim's face when Bernadette came and told him her decision.

The operation took place in September 1999. Jim and Bernadette recuperated at Michelle's house in separate bedrooms. As the weather outside grew colder, the wall of hurt between them began to thaw. A hug in the hall. A kiss on the cheek. "First we were showing admiration for each other," Jim explains. "It was love, but not passionate love. But eventually that changed.

"It was like we were eighteen again. We'd rent a movie and I'd wonder, 'Gee, should I put my arm around her?' It felt so good. We talked about moving in together and decided it would be good for the family. Besides, it was practical."

On the surface, their new life resembled the old one. Jim worked nine-to-five. Bernadette worked night shift at the hospital. But their hearts had broken and mended — and grown in the process.

"I remembered back in the early days when I was so happy and I worried something big would go wrong," says Bernadette. "Well, something big did happen: our divorce. So this time we tried to be each other's soul mate."

"We had never been best friends in our marriage," Jim says.

"We didn't know about all that," Bernadette interjects. "When you don't think someone is listening to you, your mind shuts down and the rest of you shuts down, too."

This time around they shared their feelings and put aside special time to talk. They made a special point of being honest and not keeping secrets. It felt good so they kept doing it. Then after a few years, they discovered something else had changed: their sex life was off the charts.

"The love just kept building into something bigger," Jim confides. "I had heard about falling in love with the same person twice. I never believed it. But it happened to us."

One night at dinner, Bernadette told him: "Jimmy, I never thought I would have the same feelings again, like a young girl, but I do."

"I got all choked up," Jim recalls. "I thought, *she really loves me.*"

"I was feeling fulfilled in a way I never did before," Bernadette says shyly. "And I love Jimmy *more* than before. I look at him and see that nice, nice boy I fell in love with. I see the wonderful father and grandfather, too. I call him every day and tell him I love him."

"I've changed, too," Jim says. "I have learned that you have to show your love all the time. Sometimes we hug, and just stay there, feeling each other."

A wedding was called for. In 2009 — ten years after the kidney operation — Bernadette and Jim pledged their troth for the second time.

"When you're both kids and you hear those words in the ceremony, you don't really get it," Jim says. "This time the words meant so much more." 🍁

"I opened up the hotel room door. And yes, I saw wrinkles, but there he was, the same twenty-one-year-old sailor I had fallen in love with!"

PEGGY and RAY

Long ago — well, in 1970 — a sailor arrived on an island. He had come from the dry, dusty middle of America, so to him this island felt like magic, especially when a local girl came to him and spoke her truth so simply. The sailor was shy and plain-spoken but with this girl, his tongue was loosened. In four months time, they were betrothed. Her father disapproved, however, and the sailor moved far away. He could not forget the girl, so after many years, he went in search of her. And you know what? She was now living on another island, even prettier than the first. All the feelings they had for each other came flooding back. So he moved to her island and they are happy to this very day.

That's pretty much how it happened with Peggy and Ray ... although there's a *little* more to the story...

At 20, Ray left his small town in Kansas to join the Navy. They made him an Electrician's Mate and gave him two sealed envelopes. One contained orders to submarine school; the other to Adak, Alaska. "They said 'pick one,' I did, and they tore the other one in half," recalls Ray, still astonished at the turns life can take.

He ended up on Adak, an island at the southernmost tip of the Aleutian chain. Ray was working at the Navy's TV/radio station one afternoon when an 18-year-old girl suddenly walked through the door.

"I needed a date for my senior prom," says Peggy, her smile as wide and friendly today as it was back then. "So I walked right up to Ray asked if he'd be my escort."

"I was flabbergasted," Ray recalls. "She was so pretty! And we just got along so good. We talked and talked and never ran out of things to say. By the end of the summer we were engaged."

Then the Navy gave Ray new orders, to join a ship in California. He left Adak in February, promising to call Peggy as soon as he arrived. Which he did. But Peggy never heard about that phone call, or any of the others. She was her father's favorite and he was none too pleased about her going away.

"Now all communication was through her dad," Ray says grimly. "First it was, 'she's not here' and 'she'll call you back.' Then he said, flat-out, 'I'm not going to have my daughter marrying a sailor and taking off for San Diego. It isn't going to *be*.'"

Ray let it go. He thought he had to. And all Peggy knew was that, somehow, "Ray just wasn't there anymore."

Devastated, Ray returned to Kansas, got work in a welding factory and married a girl he'd grown up with. Peggy married, too, but divorced after eight years. "After that, I just kind of kept to myself," she says. "The church became a big part of my life. I spent a lot of time praying. For someone. Someone to love me again."

"Why do Peggy and I feel so right together? It's like there are two parts to the puzzle ... and she's the missing piece."

Ray's life didn't have much love in it either. "My wife and I lived separate lives under the same roof. I never felt for her what I had for Peggy. One night — I was in my early 50s — I pulled out my scrapbook from the service. There was Peggy's photo from the prom. I wondered how she was. So I did some Internet snooping and found out she worked for the military on Whidbey Island."

"I received an e-mail at work," Peggy recalls, smiling. "It read, 'Blast from the past, don't know if you remember me.' And of course I did, right away."

"I explained to her what had happened, with her dad and all," Ray says.

"I never knew," Peggy says. "Now it seemed like Divine Intervention ... the timing of it ... my dad had just died one month before. Ray and I started writing these real lengthy e-mails, just like we used to talk so much. It was as if no time had passed whatsoever."

Thirty years after they said goodbye on Adak, Peggy and Ray met in Omaha, Nebraska, where Ray had business.

"I opened up the hotel room door," Peggy recalls, "and yes, I saw wrinkles, but oh, there he was, the same twenty-one-year-old sailor I had fallen in love with!

"That first weekend was wonderful. It was like coming home. At a mall, a young clerk said, 'Oh, how sweet! You guys are holding hands!' I thought to myself, *if you only knew!*"

Six months later, Ray came to visit Peggy on Whidbey Island. When he left, Peggy felt like her heart would break. She needn't have worried. Although it took many months for Ray to rearrange his life, he was not about to let Peggy go again. In July 2004, they were married on a boat off Whidbey Island.

"I'm not a man of words," Ray admits. "'Where's the remote' — I know that one. Why do Peggy and I feel so right together? Well, it's like there are two parts to the puzzle ... and she's the missing piece. I am just so grateful to be with my girl again." ❦

MARION and MICHAEL

June 1965: Dear Michael wrote Marion Skidmore on the back of her high school yearbook picture, *I cherish our friendship and want it to last a lifetime. Marion, there's nobody in Barlow that I like better,* Mike Inaba had written two years earlier on the back of his senior photo.

Barlow is the Connecticut high school they both attended. Marion was an outgoing girl with a hearty laugh. Michael was quiet, with an undertow of dark emotion. Somehow they fit just right together. And how they both loved to dance! They danced at friends' houses, at Marion's house, at his senior prom and at hers. When Marion went off to college, they kept in touch with audiotapes. But Marion's recorder broke after a few months. She never heard the last tape Michael sent. He never sent another. What they felt for each other became a memory.

June 2001: Marion is long divorced. She has pretty much given up on relationships. One morning her mother is scanning obituaries in the local paper and sees that Michael's mother has died. She picks up the telephone.

"Marion," she cries, "Whatever happened to Mike Inaba?"

"I have no idea, Mom."

"He was such a nice boy, Marion. Why don't you send him a sympathy card?"

Marion realizes: *I really do want to know how he is.* The reason it takes her so long — three weeks — to send the card to his Long Island address is because it's hard to strike the right note: friendly enough so Michael knows she cares, but casual enough so that if he's married, he won't feel awkward.

What Michael feels is elation. He is not married — there was just one short, unhappy union — and he thinks of Marion not

infrequently. The reason it takes him so long to call — three days — is because he doesn't want to appear too eager. On the phone, he asks her out for that Friday night, and they plan to meet at a restaurant near Marion's house in Connecticut.

Friday dawns brutally hot. After work, Michael dons a suit, buys a huge bouquet of roses and begins the long drive. Traffic is bumper to bumper. Five phone calls later and two hours overdue, Michael bursts into the restaurant in a wilted suit, carrying two dozen drooping flowers. Marion bursts out laughing: he looks so hot, so tired, so … dear. She walks over and hugs him hello.

In high school, Marion's easy affection melted the wall around Michael's heart. It had been erected against a lonely childhood. Then, after a stint in Vietnam, and years of adult solitude, the wall had gone up again. Michael's life was carefully arranged around his job, his beloved tennis and a few good friends. Now, sitting and talking with Marion over dinner, he feels a grateful amazement: thirty-four years have passed but love did not die.

"Let's go dancing," he suggests, taking Marion's hand.

"You're in Connecticut, not New York," she responds, smiling. "But," she adds, "I live only twenty minutes away."

In Marion's house, they slow dance and Michael kisses her on the neck, a sensitive spot he remembers from high school. He never makes it to his Saturday tennis game.

Marion never heard the last tape Michael sent. He never sent another. What they felt for each other became a memory...

On Sunday, Marion's 20-year-old daughter, over as usual to do her laundry, watches open-mouthed as her mother and a strange man, dressed in an old shirt of her brother's, glide around the living room as Rod Stewart sings "Have I Told You Lately That I Love You?"

Soon they have a weekly ritual: their Friday Night Date. They set out martinis and shrimp cocktails, then they toast each other, then they dance. It's just the two of them, remembering how special their connection is. Michael begins his own ritual, sending Marion flowers on the 27th of each month, because July 27th was their first date the second time around.

"One *Wednesday* night I came home from work," Marion says, a laugh bubbling up, "and it was all set up like our Friday Night! There were the martini glasses and the shrimp, plus there were flowers all over the place!

"Michael informs me that it was the twenty-seventh day of the twenty-seventh month we'd been dating. Then he gave me the ring!"

First, they danced. Then they phoned everyone. Marion chuckles at the memory.

"When I told my mother, she said, 'I always *told* you to read the death notices!'" 🍁

MILEIGH and ALBERT

Miami, Florida, July 1, 2006: An 84-year-old man with a wiry build and a white sweep of hair gets into his BMW M3 in the early dawn. He plans to drive west across the continent and then north to Vancouver, British Columbia. In spite of the miles ahead, he is eager to start. Halfway through the journey, the man plans to stop and look up a woman he fell in love with fifty-five years before.

"In 1951, I was twenty-nine years old, a pilot flying for a major airline," Albert Wells recalls. "Mileigh was a stewardess for that airline. Every once in a while I would see her and think, *Oh God, she's beautiful.* On New Year's Eve day of that year I flew to Kansas City where we changed crews. That night I celebrated … but I over-celebrated. About three in the morning I get a call. The captain who was supposed to fly from Kansas City to New York couldn't make it — could I fill in? I told them, 'I can't. I've been drinking.'

"They told me they had two very sober co-pilots to fly the plane. They just needed me on board. The clincher, though, was that Mileigh was going to be the stewardess on that flight.

"All the way from Kansas City to New York, Mileigh nursed me. I had the biggest hangover of my life. She brought me aspirin and coffee. She was so caring and sweet. I kept saying, 'today, Mileigh, but never again' and she would just smile.

"I had this strong feeling," Albert continues. "I just wanted to be with her. I was married and I knew Mileigh was going with another pilot. But it stayed with me, that trip, it really stayed with me. All through the years, I thought about Mileigh."

Mileigh used to be Millie, a tall, skinny girl who attended a one-room schoolhouse in the mid-west. She fell in love with words ("I thought 'Renaissance' was the most beautiful word in the world!") and yearned for excitement. When the requirements for flight attendants were eased — until 1950 you had to be a nurse to qualify — Millie signed up. "I was off into the wild, blue yonder," she says, laughing, "at twenty-one years old."

A year later, she flew with Al Wells and nursed him through his hangover. And shortly thereafter, Millie married R.B. Hall, the pilot she'd been seeing. It was a satisfying marriage and a good life, with Mileigh adding special touches — like the new spelling of her name — to ordinary events. The marriage lasted fifty-three years until R.B. died on June 4, 2005. After a year of mourning, Mileigh's days took on the pleasant shape she was used to: family, friends, church, volunteering. "I had *no* thought of dating," she says now. "I had a nice life."

Mileigh Hall, mother of five, grandmother of eleven, went home and closed up the Kansas house she had lived in for fifty-three years. Then she flew to Florida to be with Albert Wells forever.

Al's life followed a more colorful path. He'd left college the minute he heard Pearl Harbor was attacked, learned to fly, then joined the Marines. Flying over Okinawa with the Death Rattlers Squadron, Al became an ace known as "Lucky" Wells — he seemed to miraculously dodge anti-aircraft fire. But he didn't dodge life's bullets, some of which were self-inflicted.

Al and his first wife divorced after ten years. He was a gentle man when sober but he often drank to excess. He stayed married to his second wife for forty-nine years; when she died — on July 4, 2005, a month after Mileigh's husband — Al drank even more.

That next summer, Albert planned to take his whole family on a cruise to Alaska. "I decided I would drive to Vancouver [where the cruise started], not fly. I had in mind that I would look up Mildred Hall when I drove through Kansas City. I'd heard that her husband had died."

On July 4, 2006, an unsuspecting Mileigh was out with her family. Late that night, she went to check her phone messages. There was just one: *I don't know if you remember me or not but this is Al Wells. I'm passing through Kansas City and would like to take you out for lunch.*

"I freaked out — I'd thought he was dead," exclaims Mileigh. "Friends had told us Al Wells had stomach cancer and the news was he'd died." (In reality, Al had survived five kinds of cancer.)

Early the next morning, Mileigh called his hotel. "Good morning, Captain Wells! Of course I remember you."

"I was so excited when she called me back," Al recalls. "I stood at the entrance to the hotel to wait. I watched her drive up. Seeing her brought everything back."

"Well in *my* mind," Mileigh says, smiling, "I was just going to meet an old friend for lunch. I did remember that Al Wells was a lot of fun. Then I saw him. He said, 'Hi, honey.' And all of a sudden I could feel it was something more than friends."

Her voice softens. "It was very shortly after that we knew we were meant to be together.

"It just seemed perfectly natural. He was the most wonderful, gentle, lovely man. We talked about the same sort of things. I felt so close to him! So happy!"

"He kept telling me he was so glad he found me. I said, 'Oh, Albert, you'll meet all those rich widows on that cruise ship and forget all about me!' And he said, 'I'll tell you what Mileigh. If I meet a rich widow on that ship, I'll tell her I've got a poor widow in Missouri I've got to go take care of.'

"Two days later," Mileigh recalls, "Albert had to leave to get to the cruise. On his way out of town, he called and said, 'What are you doing?' 'Well I'm scrubbing the kitchen floor,' I told him. 'How are you?' he asked, and I said, 'I fell in love. I'm madly in love with you.'

"Every night at nine on the dot he called and said, 'Good night, sweet princess.' People kept wondering why I looked so happy. When he got back we spent five days together. I introduced him to my family. We had candlelight dinners and we made love."

Two weeks later, Mileigh visited Albert in Florida. She'd been there just a few days when Albert woke her up at four o'clock one morning.

"I had a revelation," he told her. "We're going to spend the rest of our lives together. I want you to go home, pack up, come back down and be my wife."

So Mileigh Hall, mother of five, grandmother of eleven, went home and closed up the house she had lived in for fifty-three years. Then she flew to Florida to be with Albert Wells forever. There was just one thing: he had to stop drinking. "Lips that touch liquor shall not touch mine," she told him.

It was a small price to pay, Albert concedes. "I haven't had a drink in two years. I drank off and on since I was a little kid but somehow it didn't seem hard at all. It was like a miracle."

Something like the miracle where a woman can live in one place for half a century, then move 1,500 miles away and feel totally at home. At first, Mileigh's friends called to see if she missed Kansas City. "It is amazing but I don't," she says. "Albert and I are together every minute. We are so close and happy."

At their wedding ceremony, Mileigh took Albert's hands and spoke Ruth's words from the Bible: *Whither thou goest, I will go; and where thou lodgest, I will lodge: thy people shall be my people, and thy God my God.* Tears fill Albert's eyes as Mileigh looks at him now and repeats the passage by heart.

"I think I loved her ever since that first flight," he says. "We've never had a harsh word pass between us. It's like we're one person." 🍂

"On his way out of town Albert called and said, 'What are you doing?' 'Well I'm scrubbing the kitchen floor,' I told him. 'How are you?' he asked me. And I said, 'I fell in love. I am madly in love with you.'"

Out of the Blue

*My partner arrived when I thought I was going to
live alone and sad for the rest of my life.*
— Alfonso Vega, story on p. 53

Love is for the young, the thin, the lovely, the innocent — that's the gauzy picture the media paints.

None of the people in this chapter fit that picture. They were not expecting romance to enter their lives. But they found the miracle of true love anyway. For some, it was disguised as friendship. For others, it was Cupid's arrow, zinging straight to the heart. For all, it was a surprise.

Most had become resigned to living without love. They'd been disappointed for too long or hurt too many times or touched by tragedy. At 62, Dorothy was positive the romantic part of her life was over. At 67, Manuela believed that singing on stage would be her only excitement from now on. And by 70, George had skillfully arranged his life to insulate him from feeling what was missing.

These stories show how life can twist and dip and take one last turn to deliver, out of the blue, an unexpected song.

DOROTHY and RICHARD

Dorothy Dutill was born blind. She endured numerous operations until one doctor let in some light when Dorothy was 6; now the spirited little girl was "legally blind." But her mother could not afford the expensive eyeglasses to facilitate sight, so Dorothy continued boarding at St. Mary's Institute for the Blind in Philadelphia.

It was there, at age 9, that Dorothy met a 5-year-old homesick newcomer, Elizabeth Rose, known to her family as "Betty-Ro." Dorothy took the younger girl under her wing. Soon they were inseparable.

One day Betty-Ro's mother came to visit and Dorothy ran to greet her. "I couldn't see much. But when I hugged her I knew she was going to have a baby." That baby was Richard, born two months later. "It was the first time I met him," quips Dorothy, "and the last — until I was a whole lot older."

Richard, too, was born blind.

He connected to the world through his sensitive ears, and as far back as Rich could remember, one of the happiest sounds he heard was the word "Dorothy."

When Betty-Ro sang a silly song she'd learned at school, or chattered about her adventures — like the time someone sneaked her into the church and posed her in the Stations of the Cross — their mother would exclaim, "Who taught you that?"

The answer, invariably, was "Dorothy Doo-TELL."

It became a family joke, Rich laughing and chorusing along with everyone else, "Dorothy Doo-TELL."

"I went through my life hearing that *name*," Rich announces in his stately baritone, a smile twitching the corners of his mouth. "Only much later did I find out the correct pronunciation!"

Dorothy's name, and the stories about her, lingered. But she moved away. She never learned that Betty-Ro became a Spanish translator, that Richard became a musician, that they both still lived with their mother. They never received Dorothy's news, either — how she'd married, had children, survived a stormy divorce, and moved back to Philly.

Dorothy continued her cheery, helpful way through life. Elected President of the Social Club for the Blind, she instituted an annual tradition: Everybody's Birthday Party. "So everyone would celebrate and make a fuss over everyone else," she explains.

One year, a friend invited Betty-Ro — now a grown up "Bette" — to the affair. Dorothy peered at the newcomer.

"What's your name?"

"Bette."

"Betty what?"

"Oh ...!"

The two women hugged and cried. That night Bette chattered gleefully to her mother and Rich about meeting Dorothy. Not long after, their mother died. To make ends meet, the family

took in a boarder and Rich fell in love with her. But talk of Dorothy "Do-TELL" continued to sound through the house.

"The lady I got involved with certainly was picking something up," Rich says, chortling. "She kept asking, 'Who is this Dorothy?'"

Ten years passed before Rich and Dorothy actually met. She was 62 and he was 51 when they both joined the Overland Blind Choir.

Dorothy's name, and the stories about her, lingered. But Rich and Dorothy did not meet until she was 62 and he was 51.

"All the things Bette told me about Rich, now I understood," Dorothy recalls. That winter, though she hated cold weather, she found herself shivering outside — because Rich loved fresh air during rehearsal breaks.

"I didn't expect anything. I believed that part of my life was over," she says. "And I knew he was with that other woman. I just loved talking to him."

"I did not know that Dorothy had feelings for me," says Rich. "I had feelings, too, but I was not admitting them to her, much less to myself."

When his girlfriend died, however, the first person Rich turned to was Dorothy. Not too much time elapsed before Rich felt better, than he ever had before! Just like Betty-Ro had started to like school, now Rich, in Dorothy's company, began to truly enjoy life. They shared, it turned out, the same playful, non-stop humor.

Rich made awful puns; Dorothy roared. He teased her; she laughed with pleasure. They made up silly songs and sang them on walks. And they loved each other physically with the same childlike joy. That Valentine's Day Rich and Dorothy were crowned King and Queen of their community center. "We were very just rulers," Rich deadpans, while Dorothy dashes to grab her crown and perch it on her head.

"Yes, she's principled, yes, she's honest, yes, she's moral. But above all, above all, Dorothy's … a LOT OF FUN!" Rich shouts exuberantly and flashes his megawatt grin. Being with Dorothy has given his considerable high spirits a home.

And Dorothy has found the perfect place for her boundless affection.

Helping him on with his coat, Dorothy strokes Rich's shoulders. "I really love you," she murmurs.

"Love you back," he whispers, stroking her hair. ❦

ALISON and ENRIQUE

Alison was intelligent, sincere and delightfully good-natured — but not one of her romantic relationships had ever worked out. After a while she stopped trying. For thirty-five years, Alison poured her considerable loving energy into the progressive Chicago school where she taught first grade.

The school's philosophy of authentic learning was dear to Alison's heart. Each grade's curriculum revolved around an engaging "central subject." In first grade, the theme was Mexico. Year after year, Alison read Mexican folk tales to the children seated at her feet. Year after year, she helped her students build a *casita*, a little house, and plan a gay *fiesta*. Alison never tired of these activities, because she had fallen in love — with Mexico!

"I loved the warmth and excitement of the culture," she says. "And when I finally visited there, I felt so alive."

Spending her sabbatical year in Mexico brought Alison to this decision: when the time came, she would retire there.

The time came in 2007. Alison was 60 when she shrugged off her safe-but-sure existence and moved to a town high in the southern mountains of Mexico, San Christóbal de las Casas.

To meet people, Alison posted an online ad under the "Friends" banner. And at first, she and the 65-year-old man who responded were just friends. Enrique wanted help with his English; Alison's Spanish had to improve. They started tutoring each other. Then Enrique asked her out. He felt so relaxed in Alison's company that over dinner he talked a mile a minute — in Spanish.

"Entiendo," Alison kept saying. "I understand." Later that would become a joke — *Si, entiendo!* — because she hadn't understood much at all.

But she was beginning to understand something deeper: Enrique was an unusually good man. Alison became fonder of him each time they met. On their fourth date, though, he told her he was also dating another woman.

"That doesn't work for me," replied Alison, who had endured enough romantic heartache. Only one month later, Enrique showed up to tell Alison that it was *"un cuchillo en mi Corazon"* — a knife in his heart — that they were apart. He wanted to end the other relationship; would Alison be there for him?

"He definitely wanted a commitment. That made me a little nervous," Alison admits, smiling. "But I just had this sense that a strong and good love could grow between us. So I took a romantic leap of faith — the first one in my life!"

She had leapt onto safe ground. What to others might seem ordinary, to Enrique was enchanting. "Alison was different from any woman I'd ever met," he explains. *"Su sonrisa empieza en los ojos* — her smile begins in her eyes. And I liked that she didn't wear a lot of make-up. *Ella no combia su aspecto para mostrarse diferente* — she didn't wash her face and become a different person."

Alison, in turn, was beguiled by Enrique's passion for

"Slowing down our speech ... it helps more than it hurts. Nos entendemos perfectamente.*"*

learning. "You know, he became an educated man by helping all of his children with their homework," she says proudly.

"I loved school," Enrique explains, "but my family needed help. So at age twelve I worked in a vineyard and at age sixteen in a steel factory. I married. My life was *trabajo y familia* — work and family. Then in the 1970s, I became interested in politics. My wife and I divorced. We had become different people."

Alison and Enrique, on the other hand, were birds of a feather.

"We have exactly the same attitude toward life," Alison says. "We both care about social justice. We don't need a lot of fancy stuff. And we have the same rhythms! We like to relax a lot but we also like to help others and learn new things."

"And she is so good with me," adds Enrique. "*Y cuando las mujeres sean buenas, nosotros hombres respondemos!* — when women are sweet to us, we men really respond!"

"We went into the relationship knowing we speak different languages," Alison says. "But there is a soul level at which we connect — where I'd never connected with anyone. Enrique understands every feeling that I have."

Enrique smiles. "She speaks Spanish *lentamente* — slowly. I have time to think. Slowing down our speech ... it helps more than it hurts! *Nos entendemos perfectamente!*"

"In other words," smiles Alison, "we understand each other perfectly." 🍂

KYM and ROB

"It was like coming home ... only to no home I'd ever known."

— Sam Baldwin, in "Sleepless in Seattle"

In the Mormon marriage ceremony, husband and wife are sealed together for time and eternity. Kym and Rob believed in this vision with all their hearts. There were two problems, though: they didn't yet know each other — and both were married, unhappily, to other people.

Their faith required they try to make those marriages work.

"Back then, I kept thinking I should be more patient, or more loving," says Kym, a petite blonde whose young husband had a severe form of Obsessive Compulsive Disorder. At the time, the couple was living in Orem, Utah.

"His obsessions took over. For example, I praised him when he tried to fix a squeaky floorboard," Kim remembers. "But then he took up the whole floor. Then he tore up the other floors. When I tried to stop him he became very angry.

"I'm a peaceful person. But I found myself arguing with him all the time. I got very depressed, and I cried all the time. Finally I had to say, 'that's it.'"

Forty-five miles away in Salt Lake City, Rob was also discouraged. While on a mission to Denmark he had married a local girl; a few decades later, their values were poles apart.

"Leaving was the right thing to do," Rob recalls, "but I was very lonely. Then in 1998, a friend recommended I post my photo on this website. That's when the magic started."

It was such a relief to lead a peaceful and productive life that Kym sometimes forgot how much she yearned for a "best-friend-marriage" at its center. She'd left her husband in 1988. Ten years later, Kym suddenly had a premonition: *something important is about to happen.*

"I felt it so strongly. I prayed on my knees every night and morning to ask the Lord to guide me. A friend had recommended an online dating site for Mormon singles.

"I went to look and there was Rob. He was so handsome! I e-mailed him, 'I like your picture!'"

She'd left her husband in 1988. Ten years later, Kym suddenly had a feeling: something important is about to happen.

Rob was thunderstruck. "It was like magic. Kym just appeared out of nowhere. She was so pretty!"

They spoke every night on the phone, establishing how much they had in common. Then Rob and Kym set a date for Saturday. But soon they realized they were both going to be in Salt Lake City on *Friday*. Kym had planned to see a movie with friends.

"We really wanted to meet each other," Rob says excitedly. "So I suggested that after 10:30 Friday night, we meet in Trolley Square, at the bottom of the escalator."

Thinking of her favorite movie, "Sleepless in Seattle," Kym said, "No, let's meet at the top."

The movie was one of Rob's favorites, too. "I'm a real romantic," he admits.

Friday night arrived. Engrossed in watching another film with her friends, Kym suddenly realized it was 10:30. She dashed out of the theater and ran to the escalator. But Rob wasn't there.

He *was* at the escalator, it turns out, just not the same one as Kym. "I didn't know there were *two,*" he recalls. Flummoxed, he tried to imagine just where Kym might be.

"Just as I'm thinking maybe Rob didn't come," Kym says, "I look around and see another escalator. I take that one, go around the corner, and there he is."

The moment is cemented in Rob's memory. "She gets off the escalator and says, 'Hi, are you Robert?' And I say, 'Yes, are you Kym?' It was love at first sight."

It wasn't until the next day that they were able to sit down and really look into each other's eyes. They talked the entire day — about their lives, their religion, their families.

Rob says, "I was twitterpated to the max. Never felt like that before, ever."

"He asked all these intense questions," Kym remembers. "And he asked to hold my hand. Then, that night, Rob asked if he could kiss me! Oh, my gosh, I had never been kissed like that. So beautiful and sweet, I was floating on clouds. I knew then how important this was."

Two months later, Kym and Rob were married in a civil ceremony. They spent the next year building up love, trust and undreamed of closeness. Then they fulfilled their dream: the two were ceremoniously "sealed" in the Mormon temple, for now and eternity.

That day, Rob told Kym: "My goal is that you are happy."

"He has followed those words with actions," Kym says. "My husband has taught me how to love more completely."

Kym and Rob's love came late in life, but as Rob likes to say, they are only now starting to live.

"Here on earth we're inseparable," adds Kym, "and we plan to stay that way *five-ever*. That's just a little more than forever!"

MANUELA and ALFONSO

Even though Alfonso joined the 30th Street Senior Center to learn English, his English did not improve, because he went there so seldom. And when he did appear — a somber-faced man in his late 60s, in a suit and tie — he hardly ever spoke. It was only when Manuela showed up, some three years later, that Alfonso revealed how passionately alive was the heart beneath his starched white shirt.

"*La vi,*" Alfonso says simply. "I saw her."

Now all Alfonso could think about was Manuela's walk — "like a song" — and her "beautiful face." Even as he sat at Manuela's table for lunch each day and talked with her quietly, a storm raged within.

Then one afternoon he let it all out. Manuela was singing by herself in the center's music room when Alfonso opened the door and handed her a poem: "*A Mi Musa* — To My Inspiration."

Manuela sat down. She read romantic Spanish phrases that told how seductive Alfonso found her mouth; how sensual, her lips. All of her charms, he wrote:

... *son como el oleaje del mar* (are like the swells of the sea)

que van y vienen, sin cesar (that come and go without stopping).

More extravagant compliments followed: how, as time went on, Alfonso respected womanly beauty even more, so he was able to say with certainty that:

Manuela had not expected any more love in her life but she welcomed it in gladly, as she had welcomed in everything else that came her way.

de Las flores, la rosa es mas Hermosa (the rose is the most beautiful of flowers)

entre las mujeres, Manuela (and among women, Manuela)

Molto bella, Manuela, molto bella (It's you who are the most beautiful).

Manuela was 67 when she received this poem. She had not expected any more love in her life. But she welcomed it in gladly, as she welcomed in everything that had come her way. She'd loved growing up in Puerto Rico with her large family — though they were so poor she sometimes didn't have shoes. She loved moving to San Francisco as a teenage bride. Yes, she was sad when her husband died young. But she loved raising their five, strapping sons.

Manuela did not date when her boys were growing up. And once they were grown, she did not care for the men who came around. Once she retired, what delighted her were the activities at her 30th Street Senior Center, especially the shows.

"I was finally dancing and singing for people, just like I dreamed about when I was a little girl in Puerto Rico," she says.

As a little boy in Mexico, Alfonso had only this sober dream: "To make a lot of money for my mother, who worked so hard."

Because his father died when Alfonso was 7, he helped all he could with his mother's business, making and selling *rompope*, an eggnog-type drink. He rushed home at noon recess to help sterilize the bottles; after school, he helped fill them. From the time he took his first real job until he left for the U.S. at 26, he lived near his mother and helped her out.

When Alfonso fell in love — in San Francisco, with a divorced Mexican woman who had seven children — he cared for all seven as if they were his own. In 2001, his wife died. Alfonso could see no happiness ahead.

He describes that dark time: *"Me retire de todo … como un niño … que trata de no buscar problemas* — I withdrew from life, like a child who tries not to look for problems."

Then Alfonso joined the senior center. Three years later, he saw Manuela. When he proposed, Manuela kissed him and said, "I want everyone to know how beautiful our love is. You have to write another poem for the wedding."

In December, 2008, Alfonso stood before all of Manuela's relatives in Puerto Rico and recited aloud, *"Un Ocaso Feliz* — A Happy Marriage." It tells how lonely he was, how glorious his love for Manuela feels, and ends:

Dios me puso en mi camino a una mujer para que no estuviera solo. (God put a woman in my path so I would not be alone.)

Esa compañera que Dios me puso en el camino, lleva por nombre Manuela. (The woman God granted me is named Manuela)

Y esta aqui, a mi lado (She is here at my side)

Y es la que me va a acompañar hasta el final de este sendero. (The one who will stay with me to the end of the road.)

MARGUERITE and GEORGE

On a July morning in 2001, Marguerite welcomed passengers aboard the 6:15 flight from Nashville to Des Moines and observed a man with a briefcase striding toward her on the jet way.

"He had the most beautiful smile," recalls Marguerite in French-accented English. "It was the smile of a little boy. And I knew — I knew at first sight — that this was the man I had been hoping for all my life."

The man was George Miller, a tall and trim 70, who had been switched to Marguerite's TWA flight at the last minute. He was the only First Class passenger, and Marguerite, a 50-year-old flight attendant, was assigned to that section, so they spent the entire time enjoying each other's company.

"I thought she was very attractive," recalls George in his understated drawl. "Something else, though — she was so alive and intelligent. I wanted to see her again."

George had long preferred to take life as it came and enjoy the ride. He enlisted in the Air Force, he confesses, "to avoid being drafted." To hear him tell it, the decorated Air Force career that followed "just kind of happened," as did a second, successful career in banking. Now retired, George was traveling the country on behalf of a favorite charitable foundation.

Work brought him the excitement that marriage had not. George had wed his college sweetheart more than fifty years earlier. "She was a wonderful woman and a wonderful mother," he says. "But the thing you hope will happen, that closeness? It never happened. We had drifted apart years ago."

And so on that early morning flight, George suggested that Marguerite look him up on her next trip to Nashville. "I'd like to take you to dinner," he said, handing her his card. But Marguerite returned to the galley and tore George's card into little pieces.

"I didn't want an ordinary meeting," she says. "To me, this man was precious."

Everything in Marguerite's life was hard-won. The seventh of ten children in a French-Canadian family, sandwiched between a beautiful older sister and a beloved younger brother, Marguerite always felt invisible.

"What I loved best was my classical music," she recalls. "It gave me the chance to pretend I was somebody else. I would

play the record of a Strauss waltz and imagine I was in a beautiful gown, with my hair up, leading a beautiful life."

When she left home at 17, Marguerite tried to build that beautiful life, opening small windows of opportunity with grit and courage. She studied English; it didn't prepare her for the job she wanted. She married; her husband turned out to be an alcoholic. But because of that early sense of invisibility, Marguerite felt free to correct her mistakes.

"That saved me," she exclaims. "I thought that … since I don't count, who cares! Since everyone ignores me, I may as well go ahead and do what I want!"

Marguerite got a divorce, unheard of in her Catholic family. She mastered English idioms by waitressing. She kept going.

Many adventures later, Marguerite was living in Seattle with her third husband, a kind man who encouraged her to revive an old dream of becoming a flight attendant. So Marguerite applied to as many airlines as she could find. When none responded, she assumed that at 47, she was probably too old.

Suddenly, all that was forgotten. Marguerite's husband died and once more, she was struggling to survive. "I was living off credit cards and organizing other people's houses when — out of the blue — came a letter from TWA," she says, triumphant. "They wanted me to come east for an interview!"

Marguerite had been proudly wearing the TWA uniform for two years when George Miller walked up the jet way and into her heart.

As George prepared to leave the aircraft, Marguerite gave him *her* card. Every night, for the next five weeks, he called.

The conversation flowed. And then George made a confession.

"When he told me there was a Mrs. Miller, we had already developed an attachment," Marguerite recalls. "I was hurt and scared. I felt guilty, big time. I was also angry, because I was falling in love with him.

"George told me that his marriage was not one of love or happiness. We had lived such different lives. But the more we talked, the more I believed our love was meant to be."

Their first weekend together exceeded Marguerite's expectations. "We had so much in common. He was my prince," she recalls warmly.

Two weeks later came the September 11 terrorist attacks. Marguerite was helping passengers get back home, while George, in Nashville, suddenly felt very lonely.

"I wanted to hold someone's hand, someone I really cared about," he recalls. "I wanted to hold Marguerite's hand."

On a second rendezvous later that month, George pulled Marguerite close. "I want to tell you something," he said softly. "This was a *honeymoon*. I love you."

From then on, they saw each other whenever possible. In 2002, Marguerite accompanied George on a trip to Lincoln, Kansas, a tiny town near his childhood farm. He was looking to buy a property. They were standing in front of the house in question, when Marguerite saw the future.

"*Écoutes!* We can make this into a Bed & Breakfast. I can fix it up. I will cook food people will love!"

"I thought her idea was kind of silly," George admits. "But she was so excited. Turns out, she was right."

"We had lived such different lives. But the more we talked, the more I believed our love was meant to be."

George left for Nashville, and Marguerite painted, plastered and wallpapered — in between making scores of friends. She welcomed George lovingly when he came to visit every couple of weeks. It was not until 2004 that he came to stay.

"I could say that I left my wife because Marguerite needed me," says George, his voice thoughtful. "But she really didn't *need* me. She has struggled with ups and downs. She knows how to handle things.

"No, I did it because I wanted to have a more meaningful life," says the "prince" who was himself perhaps in need of rescuing.

"It was agonizing to leave a fifty-year marriage," he says quietly. "No one who hasn't made that decision can understand how hard it is. But I did it because I felt connected to Marguerite in a way I had never felt connected to anyone."

Today, "Marguerite's Bed & Breakfast" attracts guests from all over the country. They come to experience the rural town of Lincoln, to eat the gourmet French Canadian food and to enjoy the hosts' extraordinary *joie de vivre*.

"Everything here is pure 'Marguerite,'" says George, pointing with pride at newly painted walls: red and orange with light blue accents.

With equal pride, he describes their life. "We stay connected on every level: emotionally, sexually, intellectually. We wake up, have coffee and start talking. She's a liberal Democrat and I'm a conservative Republican, so occasionally we'll drift into heated discussions," George adds with a wry smile.

"Everything we do is so alive," Marguerite says. "George teaches at the high school. He writes for the local newspaper. We travel together. We cut wheat together. We love the B&B. It is a truly beautiful life." 🍁

"We love running the
Bed & Breakfast together.
It is a truly beautiful life."

Working Together

*"Sharing the same work and having many interests in common
can greatly enhance the joys of day-to-day living."*

— Bob Byrne, story on page 70.

Work and love are the building blocks of life. If you're passionate about both, and can share them with your mate, you can bet there will be fun in store. Especially if — like the couples in this chapter — you've gone the better part of a lifetime without having such a simpatico companion.

Working side by side opens up a relationship. Doing what they loved best, Edith and Ray learned from each other. Pat and Walter had been separately doing work they loved all along; working together was the spark that ignited their flame.

Being lovers and sharing a passion — it's a powerful combination. Nanka and Bob's happiness can hardly be contained. It bubbles over into their community where they generously share their skills. Halina and Dennis have a mutual hobby that almost literally sets their souls on fire; every time they practice it, the world is a better place. And anyone who sees Edith and Ray act out their joy cannot help but smile and applaud. Upon reading these stories, you will, too.

Having a passion is great. Sharing it with someone you love is terrific. Finding both later in life: priceless!

EDITH and RAY

Edith asks her new husband: *Are you lonesome tonight? Are you sorry we've drifted apart?*

And Ray begs: *Won't you come home, my Edith. Please come on home ... I've cried the whole night long!*

He gets down on his knees. *I'll do the cooking, Edith, I'll pay the rent!*

But Edith's trim figure twirls away ...

I know I'm to blame, Ray admits sorrowfully.

But look! She's coming back. And see? She's smiling! Tenderly, Edith plants a kiss on Ray's forehead. And the standing room-only audience of seniors and guests erupts in applause.

"We weren't really fighting up there," Ray says sincerely. "We don't fight at all."

His life has followed an innocent, albeit successful, path. Ray still lives in the same neighborhood he grew up in; still sings (for sixty years) in the same church choir. He made a good living as an accountant by day and indulged his passion for theater on weekends by choreographing shows. Then his wife died.

"I never thought I would get married again, or want to ... then along comes this little butterfly," says Ray, who was 75 when he met Edith, 72, in a line dancing class.

"I saw her shaking her backside to the beat. Then I noticed how kindhearted she was. She kept asking all the old people if they wanted coffee and then getting it."

"I realized that Edith is a wonderful woman," says Ray, who, after one date, also realized that he and Edith shared the same passion for theater, especially musicals. They sang together coming home in the car from a show. Then at their glee club, they sang a duet. Next came another duet, at Talent Night in the Poconos.

Soon Edith and Ray had a repertoire of songs and movements that perfectly reflected their budding romance and bantering humor: "Me and My Shadow," "Anything You Can Do, I Can Do Better," "Bill Bailey," and "Tea for Two."

With matching outfits, they were an act! Ray loved choreographing their routines. Edith was a natural, improvising bits when she forgot her lines.

Edith had always longed to perform. But the opportunity had never arisen. "I was raised very strict. Then I went from the frying pan to the fire when I got married. My first husband ...could be very mean sometimes. But ... he never got my spirit!"

Her spirit is what lights the act. "Edith can do no wrong on stage," Ray says with authority. "If she blew her *nose,* audiences would love her."

In fact, Ray loved her. But he plans his life as carefully as he choreographs. *Would it be disloyal to my late wife,* he wondered. Then after four years of walking Edith home at night, Ray proposed.

The wedding — just like the bride and groom — was traditional, with a joyous infusion of show biz. Ray's priest performed the ceremony during the 11 a.m. Mass. Then Edith and Ray performed their "Singin' in the Rain" number, complete with umbrellas. Behind them, the South Philly Glee Club sang full-out: *What a glorious feeling, I'm happy again* ....

"We tell a little story on stage," Ray explains. "It goes like this: bad things happen in life ... but you can make a happy ending." 🍁

HALINA and DENNIS

Dennis had climbed Mount Whitney when he was 60 years old and Mount Kilimanjaro at 61. At 64, he biked up the formidable Mount Washington. He approached these ventures with easy confidence. But after two painful divorces, friends had to push and persuade Dennis to join a dating service.

There's when this gun-shy man met the friendliest woman in the world.

At their initial coffee shop meeting, Dennis — now 65 — relaxed in the glow of Halina's enthusiastic compliments. She was so easy to talk to! He also noted that at 59, Halina was slim and fit: a perfect companion for his outdoor adventures. A few weeks later, he invited her to climb a small mountain. She kept up, chattering cheerfully the entire time.

Months later, they were still dating. Then Dennis knew what he had to do.

Dennis's second marriage had lasted thirty-one years, but they'd rarely had an intimate conversation. Devastated that so long a union could hold so little closeness, Dennis secluded himself for a year after the breakup, trying to answer one question: *How did I contribute to this divorce?*

The truth, Dennis realized, was that he'd been dishonest. Terrified of confrontations, he'd never let on how he truly felt. At the end of his time alone, he made a resolution: "In my next relationship, I will share every thought and feeling."

He'd promised himself. So Dennis sat Halina down for a talk.

"Our relationship will fall apart if we aren't honest with each other," he informed her. "You might have to tell me something someday that is painful for me to hear but — "

"I do have something to tell you," Halina said.

"She looked so serious," Dennis recalls. "I waited for this terrible thing."

"I can't stand mountain climbing," Halina cried. "I don't like it at all!"

Dennis chuckles, remembering. "I was fine with that. We had this other thing that we shared — our spiritual passion."

Halina had made spirituality the center of her life years before she met Dennis. Her mother had grown up traumatized in war-torn Poland; Halina's childhood was filled with strife and tears. The notion that one could choose an attitude with which to face the world filled Halina with hope. Reading Eckhart Tolle's *The Power of Now* was a turning point.

At the time, she was a receptionist for a large pharmaceutical company. Each day, Halina "surrendered to the Now" by connecting positively with as many of the seven-hundred people who passed by her desk as possible. Each night, she tried to convey her joyous insights to her husband Murph, a sweet-natured, hard-working UPS driver.

"My husband could hear that spiritual stuff for a while," Halina recalls, "but then he'd bring the newspaper back up to his face. Or he'd be watching TV and say, 'Can you wait until the commercial?'

"And it was a re-run!" Halina wails, affection and dismay mixed equally in her voice.

Then Murph died of a sudden stroke in 2001. Halina mourned him deeply, even as she rediscovered parts of herself. "My husband was wonderful but a couch potato ... that TV going all the time drained my energy. When I lived alone, the quiet let me hear my heart. It led me to things that were spiritual."

In the self-imposed silence following his divorce, Dennis also heard his truth: the pursuit of wealth had led him astray. "My life had become completely external. I was empty inside. Feeling all thirty-one lonely years of my marriage was the most frightful, painful, experience. I call that time my rebirth."

During that year, Dennis studied Buddhism, took up yoga and read spiritual texts. One in particular made an impression: *The Art of Happiness,* based on interviews with the Dali Lama. "Now I understood that life on this earth is suffering and in order to overcome it, we have to help each other," he says.

When an old friend confirmed the change in him — "You used to be so self-centered. Now you're actually listening to me!" — Dennis knew he was on the right path.

A man on a spiritual path: exactly what Halina was seeking.

She had purchased sixteen "matches" from a high-end dating service after Murph died. "They were decent men but none were aware there was *something else*," recalls Halina, who forgot about her four remaining matches until one day when she was consoling a friend. The woman had met someone through the same dating service, but the man had just died.

"And she had no more matches left," exclaims Halina. "So I asked if I could give her mine." The dating service director agreed, then added, "I will give you one more complimentary match. And I'll personally find someone wonderful."

Several months later, the director called: "There's this new man and he is for you!"

It was Halina's last match. It was Dennis's first — and his last, as well.

Their first real date, February 17, 2007, fell on the anniversary of Murph's death. "It was like having his blessing," Halina says. "Murph used to always say, 'You should have married a businessman or a teacher.' I would answer, 'But I love you.' And I did. But here is Dennis, a businessman and a spiritual teacher."

Dennis had to be pushed and persuaded by good friends before he agreed to join a dating service. But when he did, this gun-shy man met the friendliest woman in the world.

"And Dennis," she adds, "is not like other men. No one can match him when it comes to talking about deep inner, spiritual feelings."

When Eckhart Tolle presented ten televised classes on Oprah, Dennis and Halina watched all ten together, talking for hours afterward. Talking about spiritual matters was their favorite activity. Doing it together stimulated both of them to new levels. One would experience a spiritual growth spurt and excitedly share it — like the time Dennis cared for his elderly father and told Halina how in emptying bedpans, he was learning to be humble. Or when Halina laboriously painted every slat of a fence around her house and couldn't wait to tell Dennis what she understood about being in the physical moment. The challenges they faced as a couple — whether or not to move in together, for example — they started to view as opportunities, each sharing every thought and feeling.

"I am as interested in her thoughts as I am in my own," says Dennis. "Before this, I did not know what love is. Halina is truly the kindest person I have ever met. When I see Halina, I see her soul. And that's a hell of a lot more than climbing a mountain!"

PAT and WALTER

January 8, 2001, Washington D.C. It's an icy, dark night. A small figure huddled deep inside her coat walks hurriedly down 18th Street. A man stands watching from the shadows. He steps out onto the sidewalk as she approaches.

"You don't know me," says the man, peering down, "but how would you like to enjoy one night stand?" He is broad shouldered and very tall.

"Excuse me?" snaps the woman. "I'm not that kind of a lady."

Right away the man laughs. "No," he says, "it's the name of the *band*. One Night Stand. We're playing in here and we need some more customers." He points to a sign behind him. The woman smiles and the moment turns.

He is Walter; she is Pat.

"I'm on my way to a gig myself," Pat says. "I'm a singer."

"Oh really," says Walter.

Right there on the sidewalk, she stares up at him and sings: *I found a million dollar baby, in a five and ten cent store …* He is enthralled with her "Lena Horne eyes," smoky voice and devil-may-care attitude.

"We were just so happy to meet each other," Walter says.

Late that night, Pat returns to hear him play. In person, Walter is soft-spoken and deferential. Not so onstage.

The band watches as Walter takes it slow, adjusting a dial, glancing out at the crowd. Finally he raises the tenor sax to his lips. He picks up the melody and gently turns it this way, then that, and then answers it, boldly, softly, completely.

"The music chose me," Walter says. "I've been playing since I could reach a piano. It's always been about the music. When my first marriage went south, I just took more gigs."

Walter matured early as a musician but late as a man. He never put that much effort into relationships. The one he was in when he met Pat was not particularly good; the one she was in, was abusive. And this was not unfamiliar territory.

The people who caused Pat pain were legion. A father who lashed out with sharp words and hard fists. Kids who taunted her because she was fat. By the age of 10, Pat was obese. In her 30s, she tipped the scale at three hundred pounds. Pat lost the weight and emerged a sultry beauty — with scars. With bad knees from carrying all those pounds for all those years. With rough edges from fighting back, hard, at life.

Even after she lost the weight, Pat still "felt fat," so she preferred singing backup rather than solos. But no matter where she stood onstage, music soothed Pat's soul. It always had. Now she and Walter began making music together.

"We just kind of melted and bonded through the music," he says softly. "We were buddies. Friends."

"Then, it was about six months after we met, things turned around," Pat says, her low voice thrilling to the tale. "Walter walked me to my car and gave me a kiss. This was a glorious kiss — real sexy! And I was shocked because Walter is such a gentleman. Even now I tell him, 'June — we call him June 'cause he's Walter, Junior — I *love* your delicious kisses!' They are the best in the world. Especially since there's such love behind them.

"It was Walter who finally made me feel beautiful," Pat says. "I was very self conscious because when I lost all that weight, I ended up with all this extra skin on my legs. I remember once we had to play for Carnival and we went to this little lagoon. I had a bathing suit on and Walter looks at me and says, 'I'm so proud of you. You're so beautiful.'"

"Pat has put up with all kinds of things," Walter says softly.

"I love giving her so much love … It's the most I have ever given anyone. With Pat I've learned that love is like a trust fund. The more I put in, the more it grows."

"I have never, ever, felt as loved by someone as I do by Walter," Pat confides. "Because of my history, I have a hard time trusting. So there was me, being difficult, and there was Walter, always telling me he loved me. Until finally I settled down. Four years to the day we met, we got married, on January 8, 2005.

"Walter gave me the confidence to become my best self onstage. He told me, 'Get out of the background! You're an entertainer, the real thing!' Now with One Night Stand, I'm front and center."

Every Monday night Walter and Sista Pat, as she is now known, transport the audience at Madam's Organ, on 18th Street. "This is the place to be," Pat's voluptuous voice assures the crowd while her smile lights the room. Walter glides over and twines his arms around her from behind. As he nestles Pat and moves across the floor and brings forth sweet sure notes from his sax, there is not a sound in the room — except the music. 🍂

NANKA and BOB

For two computer geeks, Nanka and Bob do an awful lot of giggling. And a lot of touching, too. Whenever you look, Bob's long arm is draped around Nanka's shoulder, or her silver head is snuggled on his chest. Or they're gazing at each other and … giggling. Because what happened is astounding, really. To have your good friend turn into your lover and then into the best friend you ever had, and on top of that you even start a business together …

Bob didn't know such happiness existed. A long-legged string bean of a man with lit-up eyes and a boyish grin, he considered that his twenty-two-year marriage was as good as he could expect. "There was a lot of conflict but we did care for each other. My main happiness came from my thoughts, my work, and what I did inside my head. I had no idea there was another kind of relationship out there."

Nanka, on the other hand, *had* pictured such an equal and happy bond. But because the notion came to her later in life, she thought her chances for such a relationship were slim to none. And with the fairness she always shows, Nanka explains that she wouldn't have been ready for it earlier.

Born in 1942, Nanka accepted the conventional wisdom that "men were smarter than women and women existed to serve them." Believing herself merely "average," she tried to assume the subservient role in her first marriage. Depression followed confusion when her husband, who was smart and personable, used any excuse to avoid being alone with her.

The therapist they finally consulted could not resolve her husband's intimacy issues. But he did notice Nanka's intelligence and how it was lying dormant. "You really can do anything you choose to do," he told her. So Nanka ventured into the workplace where a job as assistant registrar at a local college put her face to face with her first computer.

"Back then, remember, they were mostly room-size," Nanka says with a laugh. "This was one of the smaller ones, only as big as a refrigerator!" Responsible for making the computer work for her office, Nanka fell in love with all it could do. "And I realized *this* is what I should be doing."

When she left her marriage Nanka did something unheard of at the time: she left her four sons with their father. "They were better off with him," she explains calmly, though her large brown eyes reveal the difficulty of that decision. Adolescent boys need a father. He could support them financially, while she would barely be able to support herself for many years. And she would make regular time with them a priority.

Nanka tried to date. She still saw marriage as the ultimate goal. But the men she met were so dull that when — after eleven years alone — one man appeared more interesting than the rest, she married a second time.

That marriage imploded almost instantly. And Nanka decided she was through with dating. "It was painful to keep trying in an area where I found only disappointment."

By then Nanka was happily working as an information technology specialist at a large corporation in St. Louis. She gave up trying to find someone to share her thoughts with and started trying to understand herself. Nanka bought a journal. She wrote about what mattered most to her, about what she enjoyed in life. She penned some thoughts about love, too, imagining a relationship where the man would care about *her* ideas and *her* career.

Did a man like that exist? Nanka wasn't sure. The fact is, she was completely enjoying single life, what with friends, family, music, books and a solidly advancing career.

Bob, too, was advancing in his career, in the same department, at the same large corporation. He and Nanka heard of each other but did not meet until 2000, when they were put together on some projects. "We enjoyed working together — and we got results," Nanka recalls. "Then we gradually started having lunch together every once in a while."

During those lunches, the conversation was strictly casual, Bob says. "We talked about politics or social justice. Or Nanka talked about her kids or I talked about my farm."

"He was married," Nanka says firmly. "I had no romantic interest in him and he had none in me."

Even after Nanka retired, they met for lunch periodically. Bob e-mailed Nanka when his wife was diagnosed with terminal cancer and again when she died. One month after her death, Bob was heading to town for some errands. He wrote Nanka: *would she like to have lunch?*

They arranged to meet outside the optometrist's office, where Bob was having his sunglasses repaired.

"I had no expectation of wanting or needing another relationship," Bob says. But when he saw Nanka approaching him that day …

"Suddenly, something was different," he recalls. "It was as if someone had taken the blinders off! She just looked so beautiful."

Nanka laughs, hugging Bob's arm. "I had a reaction, too. I saw him and thought, *Wow, he really is a good-looking man.* The first thing he said to me was, 'Would you like to see my new truck?' So I went over and that's when he wrapped his arms around me in a hug."

"The whole day from there is kind of fuzzy," Bob says, grinning. "We had lunch. We talked about my wife. We didn't talk about us. I think we were both in shock.

"We did talk about that day many times afterward. When you have a friendship that's five years old and it turns over in one day — it's beautiful, but it's kind of frightening, too."

Both had reason to be apprehensive.

"My wife had been dead only one month. Having such powerful feelings for Nanka felt wrong," Bob says.

And Nanka thought, *Do I want to open up again to a man? That could mean having to give up whole chunks of myself.*

"Suddenly, something was different," he recalls. "It was as if someone had taken the blinders off! She just looked so beautiful."

There were months in between the next few dates, as each took stock. "But we were both so happy and astonished at the turn our friendship had taken, that pretty soon, we just wanted to be together," Nanka recalls.

Bob moved into Nanka's house. It wasn't long before he sold his farm, and then sold his other house in St. Louis. After a year, he sold his car, too. "We were relentless," he grins. "We sold everything. We were always together anyway."

What they kept — and what they now have doubles and triples of — are computers. Because when they're not giggling or watching a film or hanging out at their favorite bookstore, they like to work. Bob and Nanka decided to combine their skills and work together as computer consultants.

"I am technical — I can rebuild and understand operating systems — while she is into applications," Bob explains. "Nanka and I have complementary skill sets.

"But everything else is so similar," he says, kissing Nanka's head. "Our tastes and values and interests. We share our feelings and thoughts on everything, whether it's where to eat or how to spend a quiet moment. We both finally understand the power of a great relationship."

"Love with Bob is an absolutely wonderful feeling of safe harbor, having it and giving it. *This* is what I believed love should be," says Nanka. "And no matter what we do, we are having fun. How great is that?"

Best Sex Ever

Somehow, the notion has gotten around that people past 50 aren't interested in sex. Somehow, the idea has been perpetuated that transcendent sexual encounters happen only to the young.

Somehow, we need to set the record straight.

This book is filled with couples that are having wonderful, satisfying sex. And some of them — like the couples in this chapter — are having the best sex of their lives.

Hearing that, most people react with surprise. The image of an older body in a soaring sexual intimacy does not compute in our advertising-addled culture. These stories ought to turn that misconception on its head.

Take Nora and John. Both widowed, they had already had their fair share of sexual fulfillment. But soon they were enjoying sensations they'd never known before — in their 80s. Joan had dreamed of a passionate soul mate. When that dream came true, Joan was almost 60 years old. It was so wonderful, she wrote a book about it

Great sex is not, as the media would have us believe, dependent on flat tummies and unlined faces. The best sex comes from a deep emotional connection with a companion who resonates with you on every level. As we mature emotionally and spiritually, the chances of it happening are even better in the second half of life.

GINIA and JOHN

Both were born in 1942. Each grew up in a loving home with traditional values. Both enjoyed the free-spirited hippie culture of their youth. Before they circled back and found each other, each stretched their souls with great adventures and a little heartbreak.

John was 35 when he had an epiphany.

"I was driving down Highway One. At a point in the road called Devil's Pass, a car drifted into my lane. To avoid a head-on collision, I swerved to the right, toward the Pacific Ocean. As the car went over the guardrail, I thought, *I'm going to watch myself die.* Then I felt a pair of arms holding me — not physically, but truly. I felt calm, understanding it so clearly: everything has to happen the way it happens."

John's car teetered on the edge for a while but he survived. Shortly after, John entered a third marriage. He gave it his all, when a storm destroyed their home, John built a beautiful new one with his own hands. His appetite for sexual and emotional intimacy was greater than his wife's and John always felt like he had to hold something back — a challenge to his open and loving personality. But he considered this marriage his "lifetime try."

When his wife filed for divorce after twenty years, John had to leave both the house and the community he'd helped build. But he moved through those crushing disappointments, sustained by the lesson he'd absorbed two decades earlier: things happen the way they do for good reason.

Some time later, John looked to his uncertain future. In his journal he wrote: *I am looking for a woman with whom I can travel to exotic places and erotic spaces.*

Ginia was 18 when she happily shed her middle class upbringing. This was Berkeley! The sixties!

"It was all sex, drugs and rock 'n roll," she recalls. "I loved it!"

Ginia's life became an adventure. She married Leonardo, a charismatic sandal maker and together, they ran a shop on the island of Ibiza and traveled Europe with their children. Society's rules — like monogamy — were questioned and often abandoned.

"Leonardo told me, 'You are my main altar, but sometimes I want to pray at other alters,'" says Ginia, who was never entirely happy with this arrangement.

As time passed, Ginia became less tolerant of sharing her husband with other women. "Through the years," she says, "I grew to appreciate the sanity and stability of a measured life in general."

After a return to the U.S. and an amicable divorce, Ginia spent three calm years alone.

Then Ginia and John found each other online. When they met for coffee, Ginia especially liked how he surrounded her hand with both of his. The enveloping warmth, she'd soon learn, was John's essence.

And soon, John knew he'd found the woman with whom he could travel great distances.

John and Ginia have traveled to many places. But the most exotic space they visit is their relationship.

In the years since, John and Ginia have traveled to many places. But the most amazing space they visit is their relationship. It's a blissful sanctuary for two lusty, affectionate souls who in their youth sought to push the boundaries of stifling rules. In their late 50s — stable and committed — both say they have never felt so free.

"Our relationship is off the charts! Everything we do is just so warm and happy," John says, blue eyes twinkling.

"It's the most satisfying relationship I've ever experienced," says Ginia serenely. "We begin and end the day in each other's arms. I've never known anyone who enjoys sex as much John does."

"I had to go here and there, John had to do what he did, for us to find and be with this perfect partner," Ginia says, eyes soft with tears.

"This relationship is a gift from God," John says. "It was worth it, to go through the first fifty-seven years." 🍁

NORA and JOHN

ora and John wanted to start from scratch, just like other newlyweds. Never mind that she was 82 and he was 85. So they sold their houses and together purchased a spacious suburban home "just for us." The night they moved in Nora wanted to celebrate with a candlelit dinner.

"So I put all the candles on the table," Nora says, eyes wide for dramatic effect. "Then I discovered we had no matches. So we had a candlelit dinner — with no candles!"

She throws back her head and laughs uproariously. John starts to laugh, too, small mirthful sounds. Candles, no candles — what does it matter, really, when you're smack in the middle of the sexiest and closest relationship you've ever known?

It's not that their previous relationships were awful or their lives, dull. John, the CFO of a large charitable organization, enjoyed a long, harmonious second marriage. Nora, a professor of American literature, was widowed in her early 30s, then widowed a second time at 76. Both marriages were successful, she thought. For six years, Nora had been leading a "happy, independent single life" when John noticed her in the YMCA pool.

Actually, he'd noticed her ten years before, in the very same place. Back then John was a married man, so he'd simply observed how pretty she was and kept swimming. Now John was a recent widower, standing in the pool, when Nora swam one of her determined laps right by him.

"Lo and behold, it was this same gal," John recalls. "So I stopped her and said, 'I would like to take you out sometime.'"

Although John's presence is gentle and low-key, the philosophy he's lived by is one handed down to him by his farmer father: *Son, in order to properly plow a field, pick a point at the very end of the field and go straight toward it.*

In other words, John explains, "He let me know you have to keep your eye on the goal."

"That's exactly how he did it with me!" Nora cries in mock-alarm. "Came on strong and never stopped!"

At first, Nora wouldn't even kiss him. She feared John might be trying to assuage his loneliness "with just anyone." But John was distinctly drawn to Nora.

"I loved everything about this gal here," he says kindly. "I loved her sparkling personality. I looked up some things she had published and thought she was so smart and wise. I was so smitten with her that I proposed on the second date."

And John proposed on each subsequent date until Nora gave an order: he was not to ask her to marry him again unless she *said* he could.

Then her feelings changed. A month after their first date, they were driving in John's car when he started to sing along with the big band CD he'd just put in. Nora recognized a fellow music lover — John knew all the words — and joined her voice to his. A week later, at a formal dance, they moved to the music.

"John held me tight on the dance floor," Nora recalls. "Oh, it felt so good. When he dropped me off, he gave me three wonderful kisses. After he left, I just kind of staggered around! The next day, I had so much energy! I thought, *I want this man in my life.*"

A few days later, they went out to dinner. John said, as usual, "We need to talk about us." But this time Nora replied, "Well, why don't you ask that question?"

John shakes his head. "Boy, did she floor me. It took about ten or fifteen seconds for me to remember what question she was talking about. Then I said, 'Nora, will you marry me?'"

For their wedding, on July 3, 2008, Nora and John planned a sing-along of love songs.

"His song to me was 'Dearly Beloved.' My song to him was 'Our Love Is Here to Stay,'" says Nora, gray eyes glittering with fun. "Then the last song I had for him was a surprise: 'Oh, Johnny, Oh, Johnny, How You Can Love...'"

John started laughing when he heard it. He understood the reference.

"You see, our lovemaking goes into the stratosphere," Nora confides. "I just had never known the sensations John produces in me. And he never knew the kind of closeness we achieve. And to think we would have missed this level of passion if John hadn't spotted me in the YMCA pool!"

The days after the wedding seemed graced by their love. No worries, just fun. Just Nora reaching for the orange juice in the supermarket and John taking that opportunity to hug her. Just beaming back at the passers-by who smiled at their exuberant displays of affection. Just sitting and singing every old song they could think of to each other.

Then life—which had gifted them so surprisingly—challenged them with a start. Three months after moving into their new home, John, who'd already lost sight in one eye, suffered injury to the other. Two surgeries could not save his vision.

Six months later, John concedes, "It's a bit of a learning curve all right." The Society for the Blind has helped with computer gadgets and daily coping. Nora takes care of his spirit.

"We have cut down on travel," she says gaily, "but we are keeping up with cultural events. If I fill John in on the plot beforehand, he can follow the dialogue in a movie! I just whisper to him, a *little*. We kept our season tickets to the opera, the rep, and the symphony."

"You know, one of the hardest parts of this," John begins, starting to chuckle — while Nora leans forward, smiling in anticipation — "is when we're out and I have to go to the bathroom."

"Oh!" Nora hoots with laughter and picks up the story. "We have devised a perfect solution. I just go up to a likely looking gentleman on the bathroom line and say, 'Would you mind taking my husband to the bathroom?'"

"They are always so nice about it," she says with delight. "And John gets to meet the most interesting people!" She reaches for John's hand and they laugh together. 🐦

"I'll tell you something," John says. *"I don't like what's happened, of course. But as close as Nora and I were before, it has brought us even closer."*

CONNIE and PAUL

Connie Feutz never lacked for lovers. Neither did Paul Joseph Brown. Both had achieved lasting professional success. Neither had reached that pinnacle in romance.

In their early 50s, they were still looking.

One evening in 2008, Paul signed onto a dating website without high hopes — and then he spotted Connie. It wasn't just her pale skin and dark curly hair (though that was his favorite combination). It was a subtle something else that his photographer's eye picked up.

"There was a directness with which Connie addressed the camera," he recalls. "A kind of ... fearless clarity."

Connie laughs, a joyful little shout, and tells a story.

"I was about fourteen, a horseback rider, and my grandfather gave me a saddle for my birthday. 'That's a beautiful saddle, Grandpa,' I said, 'but it's not the saddle I want.' My parents were *appalled* but my grandfather agreed to exchange it if I worked to make up the difference."

Connie turns serious. "I always knew *exactly* which saddle, which horse, which person I wanted. Except that I never found any one person who had everything I wanted. I enjoyed a very full romantic life — but from the age of 18, I was never monogamous.

"I thought as long as I told the truth, no one would be hurt. When I look back now, even though I was honest, I know it was cruel. I would get involved but I just ... didn't ... *attach.*"

At 30, Connie married. Halfway into their twenty years together, she felt deeply alone and dismissed. "He was brilliant but unhappy. Kind to others but no longer kind to me. No, I didn't have an affair. He didn't want me to. And I can't abide deception."

Strong words, strong will. A will much like Paul's.

Paul was determined to live a life with meaning. Watching his father struggle to find a place in the world made a painful impression. "So I found something I loved, photography, and put everything into my career."

It was easy to outshine such a father. But not so easy to heal the wounds that unhappy parent inflicted. Like Connie, Paul moved from the east coast to Seattle. Like her, he recklessly broke some hearts. There were wild and wonderful affairs that brought him alive as an artist yet left him bereft as a man. He grieved when another long relationship ended, because he was losing two children along with it.

Paul tried once more to get it right, marrying impulsively at 47. Though ill-fated, the match produced another child. One of the things he cherishes in Connie is her unhesitating love for his little girl.

Connie loved her own kids so passionately that she couldn't imagine splitting up with their father.

"But finally it became clear to me," Connie says, "that I was doing my children no favors. When I left, that's when I decided: I would only mate again with a man with whom I felt a strong emotional connection."

Then she found it in Paul.

"Connie and I … we're in sync," says Paul. "In the way we communicate with our words and our bodies. Both of us have been considerably more sexually active than the 'norm.' What we have is better than what we had before. Sex is just plain *better,* when there is a deep emotional connection."

"We'd both had great sex," says Connie. "But what we have now far transcends that. I've never felt so loved and so fully desired. At fifty-three, I feel sexier and more beautiful than ever before.

"When Paul says he wishes we had met in our 20s or 30s, I tell him I'm glad we didn't. I would have loved him. But I don't think I would have recognized his tender soul. I can be much more present and gentle now than I ever could when I was younger."

Younger, they were both fiercely independent. "Now, love has shown us that the best way to heal is to move toward each other," Paul says, and recalls a recent evening.

"Connie was stressed over the day's events. After a sleep that was troubled for both of us because we hadn't been able to connect, I put my arms around her and told her I loved her and that I was there for her. We held each other for a long time, whispering assurances."

Connie tears up, remembering. "Paul is the love of my life. He is so tender, so genuine. It's like, dear God, don't you dare take him. I finally found him." 🐦

SUE and BOB

O h, you're not going to believe our house," enthuses Bob Serra, 79. After selling the one he'd shared with his late wife for fifty years, Bob bought another house — "with no ghosts" — to start life afresh with his new wife, 80-year-old Sue.

"There are *columns* between the kitchen and the dining room. This amazing *deck* out back. You just have to come see for yourself!"

The house is spotless and fully decorated — but it's no bigger, no wider, no different, really, from all the other homes on a block much like all the other blocks in South Philly. Except ... there is magic.

The phone rings and Bob proudly tells the caller, "I'll have to get back to you because my bride has just made dinner. A pork roast. And on the side is a *medley of vegetables*. There are pearl onions and little potatoes ... it's so wonderful."

When he gets to "wonderful," Bob's voice has lowered to a reverential hush. The way he says "medley of vegetables," you would think the heavens had opened to rain gold coins upon his plate. And for him, it's true.

"We laugh, we play...
inside our house, it's like
time was never born."

Born to poor Italian parents, Bob took his first job at age 11. He became the family breadwinner at 17, plugging away at increasingly challenging positions. He is proud of providing well for his family. But for many years, Bob's plate was empty of the riches he craved most: intimacy and affection.

"My wife was very ... nervous," he says carefully. "We could never get close. But I did my best to get her through troubled times." His large brown eyes fill with memories and he takes Sue's hand.

"Oh, Bob," she sighs, stroking his hand over and over. "You are such a good person."

"It's easy to be good to you, that's for sure. I tell everyone how special you are. You always hear me say, 'My wife has the most beautiful operatic singing voice in the world.'"

"It's not as good as it was." Sue's voice is wistful.

As a young girl, Sue yearned to study opera. But her parents couldn't afford singing lessons. With her first husband, she opened up a corner beauty shop.

"I liked the shop," she says. "I loved talking to all the people. But my husband had ambitions to grow. He went to Reading and had someone construct a building for a hair cutting emporium and he wound up in such debt … "

"What you've been through," Bob murmurs, stroking her arm.

"He exhausted our funds," Sue continues, "so we had to give up the business. Then he suffered a stroke. I took care of him for two years until he died." She shakes her head. "For two years, the whole time I nursed him, the only word he could say was 'sorry.'"

Her husband had been dead for sixteen years, his wife for two, when Sue met Bob in an Italian class at their senior center.

"Four months later, I got down on my knees and asked her to marry me," Bob says, his eyes glistening. "And can you see why? Look, how beautiful. And she's as beautiful on the inside as on the outside."

Sue smiles almost sorrowfully and cups his cheek. "Oh Bob," she sighs. Then she leans forward.

"Did you ever see the movie 'The Enchanted Cottage'?" she asks. "You know, the one where they are not attractive people but they go inside and they're beautiful? That's what it's like for us. We're old! I don't even like to have pictures taken anymore. But when we're together, we forget.

"Inside our house, it's like time was never born. We laugh, we play …. If we turn the *light* off, we laugh."

Sue's eyes grow wide with wonder. "I thought what I felt for my first husband was love. But with Bob, now I know what love is. It's like he and I are *one*. Please God, let us have many more years."

"You make me more excited than I've ever been," Bob tells Sue, encircling her waist with his arm. They hug one more time. Then Bob springs to his feet, his face lit up in a smile.

"Let me show you one more thing," he says excitedly. "I got the most beautiful bedroom set for us, matching. The bedspread, unbelievable. Two-tone rose colored, fit for a king and queen."   🦋

JOAN and ROBERT

Born in 1943, Joan Price was a petite dynamo who embraced life with gusto — emotionally, intellectually and physically. When life handed out disappointment, she bounced back with hope. After her first marriage dissolved, she envisioned a future soul mate and wrote in her journal: *good dancer, loves learning, passionate about sex, passionate about his work, interested in my work...*

Joan's profession was teaching. But after a near-fatal car accident at age 34, she switched subjects from English to Exercise and Fitness to convey the joy of movement. Then came another car accident — and at 50 she had to learn to walk all over again.

It was impossible to keep Joan down: she taught her line dancing class on crutches. But in her late 40s and early 50s, her love life seemed at a dead-end, and even Joan got discouraged.

"I would smile at a man and he would look over my shoulder. I had become this 'Invisible Woman' — and I still had so much love to give!"

Born in 1936, Robert Rice was a thoughtful boy who loved to paint and dance. His dream was to paint full time — but it never happened, because Robert was supporting a family. So when his children were grown, and his marriage gone, Robert retreated to a tiny cabin "so isolated even the forest service had trouble" finding him. For three years he painted non-stop. A gallery began selling his visionary work. In his 60s, Robert was finally living his dream.

One December evening in 2000, Robert wandered into the line dance class Joan taught in Santa Rosa, California. In a moment, he was part of the group, lightly following Joan's directions … except now Joan was forgetting what came next. She couldn't take her eyes off Robert.

"I saw this magnificent white-haired man with ocean blue eyes, who moved his body elegantly, obviously a trained dancer. He exuded sensuality, subtlety, sensitivity … I was a goner."

To Joan's acute pleasure, Robert returned to class again and again. But he seemed oblivious to her attempts to attract his attention off the dance floor. *Was he gay?* she wondered. *Married? Or simply not interested?*

Robert simply wasn't eager to change his life once he'd gotten it balanced just right. So a dance of a different sort began between them. Boldly, Joan invited him to walk after class in the moonlight. He agreed — but cautiously kept the conversation impersonal. More classes. More moonlight walks. Nothing other than their feet moved forward.

Nine months after Robert first walked into her class, Joan threw caution to the wind and sent him this e-mail: *Let me tell you something I haven't shared verbally. I am deliciously attracted to you. That doesn't mean we have to act on it, though if you kissed me, I'd kiss you back.* She reassured him that it would be okay if he didn't want to take the relationship further. She added: *The one thing that would make me feel bad is if you wanted to stop dancing with me!*

Robert e-mailed back that he was attracted to her, too — and he admired her courage in writing — but they didn't have to change anything, did they? A few days later, Joan flat-out propositioned him. His response made her like him more than ever.

"I don't get involved in sex casually," Robert said kindly. "I want a spiritual connection first."

Oh, this is a man worth waiting for, thought Joan. But her waiting was over. That night, Robert sent her a surprise e-mail : he was ready.

It was the beginning of an extraordinarily passionate love affair.

Joan was 57 and ready to give all the love she'd stored up. Robert, at 64, was amazed and happy to receive it. He, too, had spent years holding love in. They showered affection on each other in countless creative ways. When they still lived in separate houses, Robert picked bright flowers from his garden and placed a bouquet in the bathroom just before Joan arrived. Because his nails were rough from gardening and painting, Robert filed them as he waited for Joan in the sunshine — a signal that he anticipated what he would *do* with those hands, once they were alone.

"Robert was the man I sought all my life," exults Joan. "I found my old journal with the list of qualities. Robert had them all. Including '*passionate about sex.*'"

In that surprise e-mail when he agreed to give it a try, Robert wrote, *It's been a while for these old parts….*"

Old parts, nothing. Joan was soon having the best sex of her life, the kind that encompassed every emotion: playful and erotic, affectionate and honest. She was able, finally, to share her whole, intense self.

"I'm slower to arouse than I used to be," she told Robert, who let her know he could make love all day.

"As long as I can take food breaks," he teased.

When Joan introduced a vibrator, Robert resisted — too mechanical — but then he saw what it could do. Soon they had pet names for it, and for many of their pleasures.

A whole world had opened up. Giddy, they wondered how else to enhance this delicious intimacy. But when they searched for information about sex at an older age, all the books turned out to be academic, boring or useless. Then Robert suggested to Joan: "Why don't *you* write a book about sex and aging?"

So Joan began working on *Better Than I Ever Expected: Straight Talk about Sex after Sixty* — a spicy memoir about her love affair with Robert, along with self-help tips for senior sex.

"Do you have to include *that?*" Robert sometimes asked. "I'm a very private person."

But by then they were so in love that their highest desire was to honor the other. Joan learned to be quiet (sometimes!) and push less. Robert learned to be playful, and how to stretch his comfort zone. He believed in what she was doing.

How good could it get? In their wedding pictures — on a beautiful day in May 2006 — Joan's tiny frame can barely contain her joy. Robert's eyes brim with tears of deep happiness. Unseen is the threatening cloud: they both knew Robert had cancer.

Years before their wedding, he'd been diagnosed with leukemia and lymphoma. After *Better Than I Ever Expected* was published in 2006, Robert underwent six months of chemotherapy that resulted in a two-year remission.

"We thought we were the happiest, luckiest couple in the world," Joan recalls.

But in April 2008 Robert was diagnosed with something new: multiple myeloma, a painful, incurable blood cancer. They decided to celebrate their second anniversary a month early in San Francisco. Hand in hand, they walked the city and made frequent, tender, passionate love. They didn't know how fast the cancer would spread.

It spread fast. They never made love again.

In their wedding pictures, on a beautiful May day, Joan's tiny frame can barely contain her joy. Robert's eyes brim with tears of deep happiness. Unseen is the threatening cloud ...

On their official anniversary in May, his disease progressing rapidly, Robert wrote to Joan: *I am so grateful that you are sharing my journey in sickness and in health. When you sit so solidly in the doctor's office and listen, I know I am not alone. You are my angel. Sometimes I'm nearly blown away by how hard you flap your wings but hey, that's what angels do, I guess.*

The disease caused Robert's bones to fracture. Soon cuddling became painful, then touching did.

"We learned to say 'I love you' through squeezing each other's hand," Joan marvels. "When I touched his chest softly and he murmured, that was making love."

You are the love of my life, Robert wrote her in May. *I wouldn't have wanted to miss this part.*

In July, Joan asked him, "How can I go on without you?"

He stroked her hair. "You'll be fine," he said. "Reach out to people."

When Robert died, on August 2, Joan was felled by grief. At first it seemed that losing Robert had been the most important event in her life. Then she realized that loving Robert was the most significant. She wrote in her journal: *I found the love of my life and learned how to experience love fully. I take this with me on my path.* 🍂

Healing

"When there is great love, there are always miracles."

— *Willa Cather, American writer (1873-1947)*

Picture an arid stretch of land. Imagine clouds drifting in and a soft rain falling. After a while, bright green shoots appear. Over there, a lush blossom. Who knew?

The late-life healing — and unexpected flowerings — the people in this chapter experienced came as the result of the soft, steady balm of love.

There is no growth without effort, nor healing without intention. But love can provide the fertile field that empowers reclamation. Even if the world has cut so deeply, you've hidden your hurt out of sight. Or you've traveled so far from your original heart, you don't remember what it looks like. Love is powerful enough to remind you.

The miracle is that we are still here, after all the years of neglect. With unconditional love, Linney's creativity emerged from hiding, fully vital and ready to be channeled. Finally feeling love in his heart, David brought his long-lost part to life — and the dry land burst into bloom.

Here are stories about talent reclaimed ... self-confidence restored ... an essential nature finally inhabited. All at age 50 or older. They show that love is transformative, at any age at all.

LINNEY and RUSTY

Suddenly he appeared out of nowhere.
I turned around and there he sat,
Smiling at me, his eyes were laughing.
I smiled back and my eyes were laughing, too.
My angel appeared again and again
Until the moment when he stayed forever...

— Linney Allen, 1993

Linney was 52 years old when this poem flew into her mind. She grabbed a pen from her purse and a napkin from the restaurant table and quickly scrawled out the lines. Then she handed the poem to her gentle-faced friend, who tucked it into his jacket for safekeeping.

For a woman born with so much creative energy, you'd think this would be a commonplace occurrence. But for Linney, it was a welcome-back miracle. With the gentle-faced man — who had also lost his way in life — she was starting over.

As a little girl in Kansas City, Kansas, Linda Quinn loved to write and perform. She was passionate about books and learning. But the message she received was clear: *Girls do not develop their talents, they sit around and wait to become wives and mothers.* By the age of 18, Linney hadn't a clue what she wanted from life.

One fateful day, family friends came to visit and brought their movie-star handsome son, a recent graduate of the Naval Academy. Her parents were so crazy about him, Linney thought she felt that way too. Her mother assured her that his cold, aloof manner would soften. "But it never did ... I married a stranger, really."

As a dutiful Navy wife, Linney moved her household from one military assignment to the other, crisscrossing the country numerous times. Soon she was moving three daughters, as well. "She was wound so tightly ... you just knew something was missing inside," says her youngest, Holly. "There was no light as there is today."

Linney tried to fill the void with spirituality. She became a Christian Scientist and eventually a healer. She loved her children more generously than she had been loved. But the lonely years of her marriage exacted a toll. When her girls were grown, Linney took a long look at herself.

"I was appalled," she recalls. "I had grown ... *harsh*."

At 51, Linney left her marriage "to find the sweet, kind girl I knew was still inside."

Rusty — less introspective than Linney, far less comfortable with words — knew only that he felt adrift.

He'd grown up in New Orleans, the only child of emotionally distant parents. It was a bad fit for Rusty's intensely affectionate nature, which he learned to suppress.

"I was encouraged to be independent; that was the program," Rusty says drily. He felt ambition but could only imagine satisfying it on a traditional path. After graduating college, Rusty landed an engineering job with a major corporation and married his college girlfriend. They moved several times when Rusty was promoted and transferred.

"Everything was going according to plan, except ... I wasn't happy. Corporate life just wasn't me. But I kept my feelings to myself," says Rusty. He and his wife rarely talked. They'd gone into the marriage, clueless about relationships. "We both ended up very lonely," he says.

After twenty-five years with the same employer, finally settling in St. Louis, Rusty thought a smaller company might be the answer. It wasn't. Then his new firm shut down. At 53, Rusty was out of a job.

Rusty's malaise deepened into depression. He went to a psychiatrist but sat tongue-tied; the doctor put him on an antidepressant. Once a week, Rusty went to McDonald's for breakfast with a support group for unemployed men.

It was the same McDonald's where Linney found work, once she left her marriage.

Linney landed the position of "store activities representative." In addition to talking to community groups about promotions, Linney volunteered to pour coffee every morning.

"Oh, I loved doing that," she recalls, "going around asking, 'How are you this morning?'"

"Then one day there was this man. Such a nice-looking man. I poured coffee for him like I poured it for everyone. Once when I asked him how it was going, he said he was out of a job. I said something upbeat, like, 'When one door closes, another one opens.'"

For Rusty, the door that had opened was Linney.

"I loved her beautiful smile. I loved the sound of her voice. I sensed something deeply spiritual in her," Rusty says. "It flies in the face of logic, but it felt like I had known her forever.

"The one thing I didn't understand," he adds, smiling, "is what exactly she *did* at McDonald's. That way she poured coffee for everyone ... maybe she owned the franchise?"

Today they laugh at the memory. But their faces turn sober, recalling how close they came to losing each other.

McDonald's was the only place Rusty knew to find Linney. He was still married. He hadn't asked for her phone number. They had sat down to talk only a few times, when Linney had a run-in with her manager and was told to leave immediately. She went straight to the unemployment office, had her hand poised on the handle to open the door — and Rusty walked out!

"I got fired!" she told him.

"Let me have your phone number," he said quickly.

"I've gone from being the person who was unhappy every day to being the person who is happy every day."

Linney was taken aback when Rusty told her, during their first lunch, that he was still married. He assured her he wasn't interested in having an affair. "I want to *know* you," he said. "I think we could have something great for a lifetime."

Within a month, Rusty moved into his own apartment. He threw away his pills. Then he and Linney began to talk.

Starting at breakfast and ending at a different restaurant each night, they talked like they had never talked with anyone before. It was in one of those restaurants that Linney saw Rusty as her "angel who appeared out of nowhere," and wrote that poem.

In June 1993, when she was 52 and he was 54, Linney and Rusty married. They decided their life together would be an adventure. And what a series of adventures followed!

First they found work — together. Shampooing carpets for a cleaning company. Then, cleaning up flood-damaged St. Louis parks. Linney was ecstatic: "I got to do *boy* things! We both learned to drive tractors, in our 50s!"

"You don't know what this means to me, that we are together through thick and thin," Rusty told her. That Christmas, he had Linney's name spelled out in lights in the park. He was thrilled with their closeness.

Next, they managed a frozen yogurt franchise. They just about slept at the store, but still they had to close the doors after just one year. So Linney and Rusty took a crash course in real estate — and sold forty-eight houses their first year.

Fifteen years later — having moved themselves and their business to Arizona — Linney and Rusty relax in their backyard pool and reflect on their journey.

"We were two such lonely people when we met," Linney says. "We have both evolved so much."

"We've added a lot of things, a lot of places … but everything stemmed from the relationship. We don't take our love for granted," Rusty says. "I've gone from being the person who was unhappy every day to being the person who is happy every day." And Linney … she is just blossoming."

"What I'm doing now is learning to be an actor," Linney says. "I take classes, workshops in LA. I'm taking an improv class. It is thrilling work. Sometimes I hear that old voice, 'just sit down and be quiet.' But I work it through. I feel so connected to the Universe now, so happy."

In 2006, Linney, Rusty and her three daughters attended the funeral of her first husband; because Linney had been a Navy wife for thirty-one years, her children expected that the officers would hand the folded flag to their mother. That didn't happen. A few days later, Rusty wordlessly handed Linney an American flag he had bought, and folded in military fashion.

"That's the kind of love Rusty gives me. Understanding. Gentle. Everything I want to explore, he encourages me. Back when we were cleaning parks in St. Louis, he told me, 'The world is your oyster. You can do anything.'

"This woman who was so locked up … the flower has opened completely," observes Holly. "Their relationship is so inspiring."

"We are reclaiming all the lost parts of ourselves," Linney says. "It's so much fun you can't imagine. Our life today is like a fantasy — except it's real."

NATALIE and IVAN

Natalie's face lights up, remembering.

I'm with Ivan, it's our second date, and we're driving in the car. Then, I don't know why, I just burst into song! As I'm doing it, I'm thinking, What am I, crazy? I hardly know this man! *But still, I sing, full out: "Take my hand, I'm a stranger in paradise ...." Then I hear Ivan — he's chiming in! We sing the next two lines together. There's a moment of silence, then Ivan says, "At last! Someone who sings in my key!"*

With another couple, that moment would have had immediate intimate consequences. And the next six hours, as Ivan and Natalie sang love songs from Broadway shows to each other — both knowing every lyric — would have certainly sealed the deal. But these two were indeed strangers in paradise. They would have to find their way to each other through layers of fear and mistrust, built up over a lifetime.

Natalie emerged from her childhood needy and insecure; her father's illness left little room for the children in the family. When her father felt well enough, though, she'd climb onto his lap and he'd tell her the story of *Madama Butterfly.*

"Operas were my fairy tales," Natalie recalls. "Music was how we all related. My mother and I got thrown out of the movies when I was three, because she took me to see *Meet Me in St. Louis* and I wouldn't stop singing along."

Her first marriage almost wiped out Natalie's trademark effervescent gaiety. At 22, she thought her future secure when a charming businessman, Jewish like herself, proposed. But he was, it turned out, nothing like her or anyone she knew. After fifteen years of secrecy, lies and emotional abuse, Natalie got out. Her husband made good on his threat that she'd be "left without a dime" — worse, he obtained custody of their adopted 9-year-old son.

"I lost everything in my divorce," Nat recalls. "Everything."

Betrayed by those who had promised to help, Natalie's world view shifted downward. She developed a deep distrust of men.

"I had to start all over. I found work, first as a secretary, and then, when I was forty-three, I got a job selling computers to Fortune 500 companies. I began to feel differently about myself. I had wonderful friends; I was making good money. And I developed a solid faith in God.

"Every once in a while, I would say, 'God, I trust that you will bring someone special into my life. I'm willing to wait.' But for years, I did not date. Until I met Ivan, my work was my life."

Ivan prefers to leave out the details of his chaotic upbringing. There was "psychological damage." As a child, he was "pathologically shy."

As an adult, Ivan dated frequently but always stopped short of emotional intimacy. At 50, he was still unmarried. His career as a psychiatric nurse was satisfying. It also showed him various ways one could heal emotional wounds. Ivan was speaking at an ACOA (Adult Children of Alcoholics) meeting the night a good friend of Natalie's attended. *Wow, he would be perfect for Natalie,* she thought, and got his number.

On the phone, Natalie posed two questions to Ivan: "Do you like music?" and "What is your spiritual background?"

"The words he spoke were like a signal, as if we'd known each other in another lifetime and this was the way we would recognize each other," Natalie recalls. "He said, 'I believe in a Higher Power but I connect to the spirit through music.'"

They couldn't help but move toward each other. But the closer they got, the more their respective issues — intimacy for him, trust for her — got churned up. They tried various means of calming those issues. What particularly helped was *A Course in Miracles*.

"This is a philosophy about how love and fear cannot be in the same place," Ivan explains. "For example, the more Natalie loves me, and I allow myself to be loved, the more my fear retreats."

Natalie recalls a break-through moment: "We were at a *Course in Miracles* retreat. We had been dating four months and had never said the 'L' word. We go back to our room after one of the sessions and I was just so filled with the energy of love, I forgot to be defended and I told him, 'I love you, Ivan. I just really *love* you.'"

"For a while, we were workshop junkies," Ivan says, laughing quietly. "They were helpful. But it was life, really, just day-in, day-out loving, that brought our defenses down. Natalie and I married. We sing in shows together. We have a wonderful time, actually."

"I see Ivan struggle with his issues. But he is always there for me," Natalie says. "He always says, 'you can do it.' He brings me a sandwich if I forget to eat. All those things I did not get in my childhood, or my first marriage, I get from him. I have become a much more confident person. I'm happier now than I've ever been, in so many ways. Ivan is the wind beneath my wings." 🍁

"*We had been dating four months and had never said the "L" word. But I was just so filled with the energy of love, I forgot to be defended. And I told him, 'I love you, Ivan.'*"

RASHEEDA and VICTOR

This is the image that comes to mind when I think of Vic and me … this little girl in her starched pink dress with her two pigtails, skippin' with her rope … and Victor down the block, he's from the broken family, the boy in the neighborhood who's always in trouble. We both get beat up by life. But we circled back … and then we came together.

That neighborhood exists only in their hearts. In real life, Rasheeda and Victor began on different sides of the African-American experience: she in working class stability in Philadelphia, he in the notorious Cabrini-Green projects on Chicago's North Side.

"People like me were invisible," Victor recalls. "I was eight when I pulled groceries in my little red wagon for a dime. As a child I was shown very little nurturing love. I am almost 60 years old and I have no recollection of my family ever sitting at the dinner table with one another, not Easter, not Christmas, not Thanksgiving, not once…

"I took my first drink at age fourteen. From then until age forty-three, there was nothing. But then I went into AA. They loved me until I could love myself."

Rasheeda, on the other hand, was surrounded by love.

"To come from my family was something to be proud of. My parents taught me to carry myself with dignity. So it was shocking to learn that white folks would consider me unattractive because I was dark-skinned. I used to stand in front of the mirror and think, *I like how I look!* But 'Black Pride' was a ways off. My self esteem was really affected."

Her self-esteem took another hit when Rasheeda married, at 21.

"I expected a responsible human being like my dad. Instead my husband spent his paycheck on drugs and became physically abusive. My mother always told me that a grown person paddles her own canoe. So that meant not going home to my parents."

Rasheeda took her kids to a shelter, never dreaming she'd be on welfare for eleven years. Slowly, she put a responsible life in place. A job; then, one course at a time, two years of college credits. But her confidence was torn down from another direction, a second marriage to a man who had seemed like "Mr. Right."

"That's when I learned what emotional abuse was all about," she says simply. "It's invisible. But it does you in."

By the time the relationship ended, Rasheeda was 48 and exhausted. "After my divorce, I had one wish, to go to Chicago. The rationale was that I would get close to my sister who lived there. But mostly I just wanted to get away from everything and everybody."

Soon after her 50th birthday, Rasheeda hit Chicago. Six months before, Victor had also turned 50. But that birthday didn't hold a candle to his other anniversary: he was seven years clean. With a job and his own apartment, Victor felt hope: "I thought it might be my time to fall in love."

At the point that Victor imagined love, Rasheeda had been living and working in Chicago for a whole year. On weekends, she would walk around the lake and reflect on her life. A job awaited her in Philly. Her family urged her to come home. But for some reason, she could not leave...

"It just felt like something was about to happen to me in Chicago," she explains. "So I sat down and wrote God a seven-page letter, the main point being: *I don't know why I can't leave Illinois — but I'm going to stay until the miracle happens.*"

Rasheeda wrote her letter to God in April. She met Victor in July. They were working in the same building. One day, he showed up at her office.

"She looked so pretty, in this long African print dress. We kidded around some. When Rasheeda told me her parents had been together fifty-four years and that she had six kids of her own, something happened inside me. I invited her to come with me to the Ghanaian Festival and for dinner at my apartment."

"He made pasta, he made salad and he served me like a queen," recalls Rasheeda, smiling. "After the Festival, I went back to his apartment. And I basically never went home. He was so sweet. It was lightning fast."

"We started going everywhere together, just walking and holding hands," Victor recalls. "We went to every blues, jazz and gospel concert around..."

We're all grown up and we meet up again and he's no longer in the street. And I'm no longer looking for Mr. Right. Mr. Right looks like Victor, 'cause Victor's right for me.

After a few weeks of jazz concerts, romance and late-night talk, Rasheeda realized how comfortable she felt with Victor, and confided her biggest dream: she wanted to finish college.

"What Vic said to me, was: 'I've got your back.' When I heard that I felt so safe."

Victor grins. "I thought it would be fun for us to go together. So we both took classes at National-Louis University. Remember, I told you I wanted to carry your books?"

"We had so much fun," Rasheeda recalls. "We wrote papers together. And then we graduated together."

"I call Chicago my healing city," she says happily. "Chicago is where I realized my dream of being a college graduate. Chicago is where I met Vic. Chicago is where I began feeling good about myself as a woman."

She turns to Victor. "You know, I never felt pretty or beautiful until I met you. All those first weeks, you would say, 'Hi, beautiful' or 'Hey, cutie-pie' or you'd tell me how attractive I was. You just kept repeating it."

"Well... you're a very pretty woman! You're not even aware of all the people who give you a second look. Me being your husband, I'm aware...."

Being Rasheeda's husband, Victor tells her, is an amazing thing.

"I just never ... belonged anywhere before. Now I am blessed. You belong to me and I belong to you."

"You also belong to the whole family, Vic," Rasheeda says softly. "My kids love you. And oh my gosh, my father is crazy about you..."

Victor grins. "At first I was afraid to meet him. He is the *man*. And because I grew up on the streets, I thought he'd want nothing to do with me..."

"Hah! Now I stay home and Vic goes to visit my parents. He calls them 'Paw' and 'Maw.' My dad calls Victor his 'eldest son.' They hang out for hours..."

"It's amazing how loving Victor is considering how little love he was given," Rasheeda marvels. "On Valentine's Day he had rose petals leading from a bubble bath to the bedroom. If he is going to the store, I'm going to get a little cake or a little flower when he comes home. He brings me coffee and breakfast in bed ... we start out cuddling every morning. Then we do a meditation."

"I found out what love was when I came into the program," Victor explains. "But I never felt it for another person until Rasheeda. We are people from two different backgrounds brought together by the grace of God." ❧

DAVID and JIM

David had created a successful life. He and his wife were physicians with two showcase homes and four beautiful children. The kids were growing up smart and healthy. David's garden won prizes. Why — at a time when he should be enjoying all this — was David beset with depression, anxiety and an early alcohol problem? Why, in his mid-40s, had he been diagnosed with coronary heart disease?

His consulting cardiologist had a thought.

"I have noticed," the doctor said, "that men who have these types of problems in their younger years usually have issues in their spiritual core. Is that you, David?"

There was a part of David's nature he had stuffed down and ignored. He had sailed for safer shores. But here it was, whispering in his ear.

David thought that he might love men, not women.

How could he figure this conundrum out now, and risk collapsing his whole life?

David had repressed those thoughts as long as he could remember. Kids in school sensed a difference, though. And David had found a certain strength in setting himself apart.

He recalls: "I was about ten years old, standing in the school playground. I knew I wasn't going to get picked for soccer. I felt no one liked me. Other boys bullied me horribly. And I just decided not to care anymore. I got this sense … I could take care of myself.

"It was a defense. But it did help me survive; the teasing didn't hurt as much. I became more of a loner."

Then, when he was 25, he had his first sexual experience with a woman and felt "almost normal — even happy." *Maybe I'm not this deviant loner*, David thought, and took what seemed the next step: he got married.

Marital intimacy shortly fell by the wayside, however; it had never felt very complete to David, anyway. Twenty years went by during which he was not sexual at all. He took the feminine energy he couldn't use sexually, and passionately nurtured his children, his patients and his garden. This was not a solution; David's masculine and feminine sides felt like they were at war. Then came the anxiety, the depression, and the stopping by bars at night. When the cardiologist spoke, David listened.

He joined a men's group and began to tentatively share his secret.

"My attitude was, 'I can *sort* of recognize that I have some attraction to men — but I have a family and a wonderful life and I don't want them destroyed...'"

Then David met Jim. He was at another men's group, all set to float some more trial balloons, when he heard someone make a lighthearted joke about sex.

"I turned and there was this sexy, smiling man. I knew he was older than me — I found out later he was fifteen years older — but he seemed younger. And *happy*. I was spellbound," recalls David.

David asked Jim out for coffee.

"I found I could talk to Jim about absolutely anything," David says. "And I was falling in love, in a way I had never felt before. I told Jim, 'I want to have a sexual encounter.'"

"Are you sure?" Jim asked. "Because it might well have seismic repercussions."

Born in 1938, Jim believes one reason he became a therapist was because his own identity was so buried. "When I was younger, I never even formed the question, 'Am I a homosexual?' The way the world was back then, it would've been a death sentence."

Jim was teased a lot. His naturally ebullient personality became withdrawn at times. But it sprang back — Jim loved life. His adult years were rich with an abundance of friends, a growing career and a perfect marriage. "Except for the thing that was missing," Jim recalls ruefully. "My sexuality."

Then in the 1970s, the gay rights movement burst onto the scene. Jim decided, *I'm sick of this mess and confusion. No matter what, I'm going to face it and figure it out.*

After one sexual encounter, there was nothing to figure out.

Jim recalls: "The experience was so shatteringly beautiful, I knew, *this* is what was wrong. *This* is who I am."

He had one long affair, and a second — both satisfying sexually but not emotionally. Then, for almost twenty years, Jim was alone.

"I just thought, well, this is a good life. I've got my family, my career, my adventures. I was rationalizing. Down deep, I longed to love someone and be loved. Then David and I fell in love. It took us both by storm."

"I was in such a deep hole," David reflects, "it took a man of Jim's quality to pull me out. It took love."

Once David connected with Jim, he was not only happy but his whole being seemed to come together. Effortlessly.

"My essential energies were unlocked. I was overjoyed. Never in my life had I known anything remotely like the sense of intimacy I started having with Jim," he says.

And his fear of destroying his life?

David bursts into tears. "Totally the opposite happened. One of the most wondrous things to come out of this, is I now have wonderfully intimate relationships with my children. I've learned the more honest I am with myself, the better relationships I have with others."

"I have learned … that the more honest I am with myself, the better relationships I have with others. Including my children."

The tears continue, but they are happy ones. "During those years before I met Jim, I was on automatic. This relationship has given my life a richness beyond compare. In my medical practice, I've become a sort of 'wise elder,' much more compassionate than I used to be.

"Now my body and my soul are integrated. Which brings me to the place where I can say in all honesty, I have never loved another person as much as I love this man."

It's an awakening for Jim, too.

"I am finally doing it, finally loving and caring for someone deeply. And I'm learning to receive love … at seventy years old."

The other morning, Jim awoke out of sorts, a bit depressed. He was sitting out on the porch and David came looking for him. Just as Jim was thinking, *Oh, he's going to want to know why I'm in a bad mood,* David simply went over and sat by him.

"David was just so … present for me. It blew me away … To have someone so completely with me, in every way. This life we have is a continually expanding doorway… with our love for each other and being our true selves."

"It has been an amazing unfolding," says David. "These five years have been the happiest of my whole life."

CAROL and WARREN

Do you want to IM?

Carol considered the request. All she could see was a tiny photo of a man smiling for all he was worth. Something about him said "brave and open-hearted." Carol clicked *Yes*.

It was early December 2006. The 62-year-old editor had only recently learned what an IM was (an instant message, like e-mail, except in real time). She loved learning new things these days.

Not long before, all the new situations Carol found herself in had been frightening. In her mid-50s, she had gone from being a middle-class wife, mother and therapist to a drug addict with no place to live. But now mis-adventures had blessedly turned to adventures, leading to an unexpected new life: Carol owned her own home in a community she cared about, surrounded by friends. She had changed careers and now edited the local newspaper.

Smiling, she followed the lines popping onto the screen. Warren from Denver, Colorado, had already told her he thought she was pretty — from her online photo — and now he was cracking a joke. He was funny. A bit outrageous. This was her speed and Carol laughed out loud, typed something silly back. And they were off, on a whirlwind courtship conducted entirely in midair.

A week later, Warren from Denver brought up the subject of visiting Carol in Philadelphia.

Her response was to tell him a story.

Carol's head was filled with stories. Growing up in an unfriendly environment that starved her intense soul, she nourished herself with words. *Anne of Green Gables*, the *Betsy-Tacy* series, she re-read them over and over, books that talked about love. Later, she read everything in sight. When she felt comfortable with someone — and wanted to say something meaningful — often a story would come to mind. And then she would share it, as if introducing an old, wise friend.

Now she found herself sharing with Warren the plot of a short story she'd read in high school …

A writer goes on vacation and breaks his leg. Stuck in a dreary boarding house, he anticipates the long, boring weeks of recovery. To distract himself, he writes to a friend back home. Taking liberties, he invents a more pleasant environment: a rambling seaside inn, a kind innkeeper, the innkeeper's beautiful daughter, Margery Anne. Intrigued, the friend writes back with questions. Happily, the writer supplies new dramatic twists: Margery Anne plays Chopin on the piano at night and weeps; she is lonely for love. Back and forth the correspondence continues — until the writer receives an urgent telegram: "Reserve a room at the inn! I'm coming up! I have fallen in love with Margery Anne and mean to marry her!" The last lines of the story are the writer's sober reply: "Stay where you are. There is no inn. There is no kind innkeeper. And there is no Margery Anne."

Absorbed in typing, Carol was startled to see her screen break up. Warren's IM interrupted her: *There IS a Margery Anne. You just have to believe.*

Who is *this person,* Carol wondered.

Who he was: a shy, stubborn, sensitive soul raised in a loving, protective home. An electrical engineer by training. A devoted father and husband — until age 43, when his protests over unfair treatment at work snowballed into a legal nightmare. Warren became obsessed with his case. His children withdrew from the angry man he'd become. His wife divorced him. He never again worked as an engineer.

Warren found solace in literature and philosophy. He thought of himself as a rebel. But inside, he was still a sensitive, loving man, with no one to love. He would walk his dogs at night and think, *How did I end up alone, me of all people?*

Carol realized they were alike: both their lives had crashed and burned, leaving just the essence of who they were.

For her, it was the luckiest thing that had ever happened.

Blessed with many talents — verbal, artistic, musical — Carol was born into a family that valued only appearance. Developing those talents always felt like a luxury she could never afford. When an art professor told Carol she was the most gifted student he'd ever seen, her tongue-tied reaction was to long for a world she could not enter. Chronic and painful anxiety developed as her identity did not. The anxiety would become the factor around which she organized her world.

She married a good man except — barely 20 — she was still a child. Two daughters brought her joy. Work never did. In a series of "helping professions," she felt bored and out of place. The anxiety dogged her until — one day — a magical solution appeared, in the shape of tiny lavender pills. But they created a host of other problems.

In her 40s, Carol became addicted to tranquilizers. At age 55, the nightmare began: she found herself unemployed, in debt, heartbroken at her last marriage's demise — and out of gas for the kind of pretending she had previously used to get by.

She was also out of pills.

It was the turning point of her life. First came Narcotics Anonymous meetings, where she met amazing, courageous people. Then Carol had to come out of hiding — and rely on her brains and talent at last. Sketching portraits at fairs earned money for rent. Writing stories for the local paper provided extra income. When that turned into a job — staff writer, then editor — it was the first time she didn't have to sit on her intensity in a job. The anxiety disappeared as Carol covered stories, learned about the community and article by article, connected to the world again. This time, for real.

Carol was 55 when she got clean; 57 when she bought a home; 59 when she and three others founded another newspaper, *The Spirit*. Before, life had seemed possible only with a man by her side. Now life seemed good all by itself.

"If I'm ever with someone again," Carol said to her therapist, "I would like it to be someone whose *spirit* I love. That's what I want most."

In December 2006, she found herself e-mailing back and forth with a man whose intense spirit was bursting from the computer screen.

It finally occurred to me, wrote Warren, *that everything that's happened in my life happened in order to lead me to the Great Connection, my Kindred Spirit ... YOU! I have always unconsciously yearned for you. Now I consciously do so.*

Later they would label this time, 'Emailea Land.' A place where anything was possible. Where Warren, who was not comfortable with words, would express himself in soaring phrases. Where painful memories didn't stop them from imagining a cloudless future.

Carol sent Warren a Chanukah gift: *The Velveteen Rabbit.* This children's book by Margery Williams describes the transformative power of love. A stuffed toy rabbit is tattered and torn from his journey through life — but the best thing happens to him: he becomes Real, because he is loved.

The copy Carol had was old and tattered. She inscribed the front page: *In the hopes of being just who I am with you, I'm sending you this Chanukah present as is.*

Warren bought a ticket to fly into Philadelphia early in January. They exchanged thoughts online, how their magical correspondence would end once they met in person.

I'm taking a last walk around Emailea Land, typed Carol on January 12, after she knew Warren's plane had left Denver, *What a place!*

The reality was not as smooth as Emailea Land. But it turned out to be more magical, in the end.

Warren had brought baggage with him — twenty years of pain that had never been given a proper airing. And old issues that Carol thought she had put to rest raised their fearful heads. So for a while — to their great surprise — there were arguments. But slowly, they laid down their defenses. Good things began to happen.

Life began to change.

She realized they were alike. Both their lives had crashed and burned. For her, it was the best thing that had ever happened.

Some changes were needed. Warren got in touch with his daughters. He got back in touch with how much he loved them.

Some changes were additions: Warren had an older sister, Nadyne, with whom Carol would have been friends anywhere. They became devoted to each other.

Some changes were subtle. One day, two years after Warren moved in, in the middle of a conversation, Carol realized her insides felt different. She didn't feel compelled to argue even though they were not agreeing about a certain point.

Day after day, Warren had loved her, even as she had tested him. Day after day, he'd been accepting and patient. Now she felt a warm safe bottom floor that she wouldn't fall through.

Oh, so this is what it feels like to be loved unconditionally. I knew the words, I knew the books ... and now I know the feeling.

Just six weeks after their first IM, Warren was already imagining what their life together would look like: *You are writing a book. I'm in another room reading the newspaper, quite content, because you make me feel that way. I will go to the grocery, then I'll come home. We'll discuss today, tomorrow, last year and next year, and we'll touch again ...*

Every once in a while Warren reminds Carol that there IS a Margery Anne.

And he's right. She wrote this book. 🍂

Addendum

After interviewing over sixty couples who found love in later life, this is the image that emerges: autumn love is the exquisite moment at the intersection of the fading body and the seasoned soul. Or, as one of the men said, "Fifty is a perfect age to start looking for the person to share the rest of your life with."

He said that in response to questions I sent everyone in this book: *What advice would you give to people over 50 who are looking for love? What have you learned about love from this late life relationship?* The respondents were aged 51 to 87, but their answers overflowed with a level of jubilance a teenager might envy. "If you are given a second chance at love like we were," one couple wrote in a joint reply, "then give it everything you have." In the following pages, you can taste a sampling of the couples' responses. The rest of the feast can be found online, at www.autumnlove.org.

Words of Wisdom

You should not think because you are older, you don't have
the right to feel the beautiful emotion of love.
And while you are waiting, open your heart to life.
— Manuela Pennes, story p. 53.

We asked each couple: *What advice would you give someone over 50 who is looking for love?* None of the answers pointed to the best dating site or updating your wardrobe. The responses were almost all about attitude. That should tell us something! Our couples recommend you put these practices into place.

1. Love yourself

We hear this phrase so often, it's hard to hear it as anything but a cliché. Nonetheless, *it was the number one piece of advice* coming from people who have successfully achieved a great relationship later in life. And some of these people were not so terrific at loving themselves in their younger years.

In the first half of life, it's easy to defer loving oneself. That time is taken up with child rearing and career building and the busy-ness of living. Some of us acquired healthy routines during those years; others got into the habit of neglecting body, mind and soul. After 50 is a great time to start loving yourself full-out.

"Take care of yourself in all aspects," says Pat. "As you love yourself, you can love another."

"Be your own best friend," says Joan, who used to send herself flowers on occasions a boyfriend might. "Inner peace and contentment are contagious."

"Love yourself and love will find you," says Walter.

"Keep fit. Find activities that you are passionate about," says Esther. "These will remind you how special you are."

2. Get to really know yourself

You may have spent years trying to please your parents or your children or your boss. Now it's time to indulge — get to know yourself in full, delicious detail. Those are marching orders, from every single couple! In Vernon's story we see that he achieved worldly success but wasn't able to truly love until he'd thoroughly explored himself. Take as much time as you need.

"Get to know what matters most to you," says Nanka, who stopped dating and started journaling. "Get to know your deepest values. Find out what principles you will not compromise, what your deepest thoughts are, what you really love. By the time I met Bob, I knew who I was and could be fully present."

3. Look clearly at the past

"Before you jump into another relationship, be complete with the one you've left," says Ron. "If I hadn't done that, I don't think my relationship with Basia would be as good as it is."

"Make peace with yourself about past relationships that didn't work," says Basia. "See your own unworkable patterns and rise above them."

4. Create a life you love

It's a win/win. The more positive a life you create for yourself, the more you'll attract positive people into your life.

"Create a life that feels right to you, with friends, activities, places of community that nurture you and foster contentment," says Dorothy. "Be happy and more happiness will follow."

5. Take a risk; be open to opportunity

"Reach out to someone you were fond of in your past," advises Marion. "The risk I took to contact Michael was the best thing I ever did."

"Your soul mate could be standing next to you in line at the market," says Wanda. "Smile and feel positive."

"Don't be afraid to talk to strangers," says Nora, who was 82 when she struck up a conversation with John in a swimming pool. "Talk to strangers on elevators, on planes, in restaurants!"

Linney met Rusty at McDonald's; Marguerite and George met on a plane; Pat and Walter met on the street. Be open.

6. Get out there in the world

Dorothy and Rich sang in the same choir; Basia and Ron went to the same talk; Edith and Ray took the same line-dance class, as did Joan and Robert. Bob and Sue met in their Italian class! And Alison and Enrique started out tutoring each other.

"Participate in social activities that you love and you'll meet people with similar passions," says Joan.

7. Be creative and thoughtful when choosing a partner

"Your interests and desires have changed," says Ken. "Look for what you want now."

"Choose someone you can be yourself with," says Dennis.

"You have so much more to share now," says Rasheeda.

"Don't settle," says Connie. "Don't fall into the belief that, 'Gee, I'm fifty-five or sixty, the pickings are slim. Picture what you want in a partner and have faith you'll find it."

8. Don't give up

The universe of possibilities is endless — believe!

"It may be easy to get discouraged after a divorce or a loss," says Rob, "but don't give up."

"Be patient. Love comes in all shapes and sizes," says Jim. "It will come when you least expect it."

"You are not alone," says Enrique. "In the world, without doubt, there are other people like you."

"Don't give up," says RJ. "You never can tell what life holds in store."

For more Autumn Romance *survey responses, please visit www.autumnlove.org.*

Advantages

A love affair that starts later in life can be far superior
to one that happens in the earlier years.
— Bob Byrne

Ah, romantic love — the province of youth. But what about autumn love? Can it survive doubting friends, protective family, the ever present ticking of the clock? The answer, revealed in more than sixty interviews, is a resounding *Yes!* Time may not be on our side, but now love arrives with a richer, deeper patina. What are its advantages? Our couples count the ways.

1. Time

When you're not rushing to take kids to soccer and build a career, there is more time to devote to a *relationship*.

"There is time for every day to be about the two of *us*," says Bob S. "Knowing that Sue is close by all the time fulfills a dream I had when I was young."

2. Living in the moment

You've possibly suffered enough losses, and seen how quickly time evaporates, to know about cherishing the present.

"We value every word, every gesture, every touch. We are very aware that life is short!" says Susan.

3. Wisdom

Oh, the lessons you've learned! You can now apply all this wisdom; love relationships in particular will benefit enormously.

"The years have given us perspective on what's important and what is not," says Edith.

See more thoughts from our couples at www.autumnlove.org!

4. Self-knowledge

You've developed your strengths. You know your weaknesses. Not only do you well understand who you *are*, you're comfortable in your own skin and can revel in sharing that.

"By now I know my inner needs and how to get them met," says Kym. "So that frees my desire to fulfill my companion's needs."

5. Correcting past mistakes

Everyone has made relationship mistakes. Here is an opportunity to do things differently. The majority of couples said they are more accepting, more patient and less judgemental. Many shared that they used to try and change their partner; now, they try to improve themselves.

"I now know the value of attention and affection," says Rusty. "I take the time."

"I am listening better," says Halina. "I try and focus clearly on what he is saying, rather than what my response will be.

"I try and communicate more," Michael says.

6. Gratitude

Remembering what it was like to be lonely ... or in a loveless relationship ... heightens your sense of gratitude. And gratitude elevates your sense of enjoyment. You will simply be happier.

"Rusty and I express our gratitude for our love every single day," says Linney. "We leave notes on each other's pillows. We remember the past, and we don't forget how lucky we are!"

The Photographers

Keith Angelitis

Being involved with this project made me feel good about getting older. You truly are as old as you feel if you stay true to your self and young at heart. Keith Angelitis is a freelance photographer in Philadelphia. www.angelstudios.org

Esther and RJ, pp. 26, 29, 118; Rasheeda and Victor, pp. 103, 122; Marion and Michael, p. 122; Sue and Bob, p. 118.

Rodney Atienza

For a freshly married man, this was an incredible opportunity for me, to get to know these couples and hear their wisdom and life experience, then bring it back to my wife. Rodney Atienza is a photojournalist based in Philadelphia who has focused on issues of social concern for 15 years. www.rjaphoto.com

Halina and Dennis, pp. 3, 64, 65, 67; Basia and Ron, pp. 13, 14, 118; Bernadette and Jim, p. 30; Marion and Michael, p. 37; Pat and Walter, pp. 69, 121; Nanka and Bob, pp. 70, 73, 118; Nora and John, pp. 78, 79, 81; Linney and Rusty, pp. 94, 97, 98; Natalie and Ivan, pp. 100, 101, 121, 122; Rasheeda and Victor, pp. 105, 118; David and Jim, pp. 107, 108, 109, 121; Susan and Ed, p. 122.

Rebecca Barger

Love is so much more than a physical thing, however, love reveals itself physically. Working on this project was a wonderful contrast to the young, couples I photograph! Rebecca Barger traveled the world as a staff photographer for The Philadelphia Inquirer, acquiring two Pulitzer Prize nominations; she is a wedding photographer in Philadelphia. www.rebeccabarger.com

Susan and Ed, p. 21; Dorothy and Richard, pp. 42, 44, 46; Sue and Bob, pp. 84, 85; Carol and Warren, p. 111.

Marian Brickner

What a heart warming opportunity for me to be able to photograph "older" couples for this important book! Marian Brickner, born in 1937, became a professional photographer in her 50s. marianbricknerphotography.com

Linney and Rusty, p. 92, 121; Nora and John, p. 122; Nanka and Bob, p. 127.

Paul Joseph Brown

Not only did I get to photograph a great couple, but soon it became clear that my partner and I should be subjects for the book as well! Paul Joseph Brown is a Seattle-based freelance photographer after 30 years as a photojournalist. www.pauljosephbrown.com

Peggy and Ray, pp. 33, 35; Connie and Paul, p. 82.

Tanja Butler-Melone

Meeting Judy and Vernon, you could just see that this was their right time and place. I feel honored to have been asked to capture the special love they share. Tanja Butler-Melone, the owner of Contemporary Expressions Photography in Denver, Colorado, specializes in casual, artistic, refreshingly unique portraiture. www.contemporaryexpressions.net

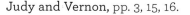

Judy and Vernon, pp. 3, 15, 16.

Bonnie Charleston-Stevens

I was delighted to be involved in this project because the topic is so very dear, untapped and important. Bonnie Charleston-Stevens specializes in portrait, commercial and freelance photography in the Philadelphia area. www.charlestonstevens.com

Edith and Ray, p. 1; Halina and Dennis, p. 122.

Joyce Harlow

People assume passion is only for the young, George and Marguerite shatter that theory. **Joyce owns the Harlow Studio & Gallery in Lincoln, KS, since 1986. www.harlowstudio.com**

Marguerite and George, p. 56.

Andrew Milne

It's always gratifying to see that you have captured something special between two people. **Andrew Milne is a freelance photographer based in Fort Lauderdale. www.andrewmilnephotography.com**

Mileigh and Albert, p. 39.

Jack Nelson

Alison and Enrique's story is an inspiration. Love is always a miracle, but to have it happen later in life makes it all the more special. **Jack Nelson is a graphic designer, photographer and filmmaker in San Cristobal de Las Casas. www.jack-nelson.com**

Alison and Enrique, pp. 49, 121.

Mitch Rice

To be able to capture the joy and love shared by Joan and my father was a pleasure. Their love came through in the photographs so clearly. **Mitch Rice Studios, in Santa Rosa, CA. www.mitchrice.com**

Joan and Robert, pp. 87, 89, 90, 91, 121.

Adam Shane

Love is such a blessing that no one should be deprived of it at any stage. I'm so glad to have been a part of bringing these stories to light. **Adam Shane is a professional freelance photographer based out of Las Vegas and Los Angeles. www.adamshane.com**

Wanda and Bob, pp. 23, 24.

Chela Shanti Richheimer

It has been an honor for me to be involved with this project. Each couple allowed themselves to be vulnerable in front of the camera, something that takes a lot of courage, and for that I am very grateful. **Chela Shanti Richheimer is a Bay area photographer who spends way too much time photographing her own two sons, ages 6 and 9. chelashantiphoto.com**

Manuela and Alfonso, pp. 3, 53, 54, 118; Ginia and John, pp. 74, 77, 121; Sally and Ken, pp. 8, 9, 11, 121.

Dena Sorensen

What I liked especially that this project is that it celebrates the timeless nature of love. **Dena Sorensen is a studio and natural light photographer located in Denmark, Kansas. www.denasorensen.com**

Marguerite and George, pp. 57, 59, 60.

Alisha Stamper

Not giving up on finding love, regardless of one's age — this is beautiful to see and a bonus to document. **Alisha Stamper holds a BFA in photography and focuses on women's activist work. She lives in Salt Lake City, Utah. www.alishastamper.com**

Kym and Rob, pp. 51, 52, 118.

Kevin York

I was happy to help with this project because it is about the power of love. As a photographer, I try to say 'I love you' one image at a time. There is no doubt that this book is saying to the world "I love you." **Kevin York is a professional wedding photographer based in Philadelphia. www.kevinyorkphotography.com**

Edith and Ray, pp. 2, 62, 63; Carol and Warren, p. 112, 115.

Celebrating Seniors And Making Dreams Come True

Autumn Romance and Twilight Wish®

Every time a copy of *Autumn Romance* sells, life gets better for a deserving older person — because part of the book's profits are being donated to Twilight Wish, a nonprofit 501(c)3 organization established in Pennsylvania, and growing to serve nationally.

Twilight Wish enriches the lives of seniors through individual wish-granting celebrations — a way of giving thanks to those who now live quiet, humble lives. Every day, some 3,500 people turn 85 in our country. Twilight Wish facilitates wonderful ways to acknowledge and honor them.

Wishes granted range from simple items, such as clothing, to vital necessities, such as hearing aids. Sometimes seniors dream of seeing a family member or their home town; other times they would thrill to re-live a day in their former profession, or to meet a favorite professional athlete or other long-admired person.

As couples in this have book discovered, we all have to work together, and help each other, to mitigate life's difficulties. Purchases of *Autumn Romance* will help Twilight Wish achieve its mission and help make our culture a nicer place to age one wish at a time..

If you'd like to learn more about Twilight Wish:
www.twilightwish.org
angels@twilightwish.org or 1-877-893-9474.